Explorers for God

NATHAN AASENG

ILLUSTRATED BY
DOUG OUDEKERK

Augsburg
MINNEAPOLIS

Family Read-Aloud Collection
Foreword by Walter Wangerin, Jr.

VOL. III

EXPLORERS FOR GOD

Text copyright © 1998 Augsburg Fortress.
Illustrations copyright © 1998 Douglas Oudekerk.
All rights reserved. Except for brief quotations in critical articles or reviews, no part
of this book may be reproduced in any manner without prior written permission
from the publisher. Write to: Permissions, Augsburg Fortress, Box 1209,
Minneapolis, MN 55440.

Scripture quotations are from the New Revised Standard Version of the Bible,
copyright © 1989 by the Division of Christian Education of the National Council
of the Churches of Christ in the U.S.A. Used by permission.

Cover design by Craig P. Claeys
Text design by Lois Stanfield, LightSource Images

Library of Congress Cataloging-in-Publication Data

Aaseng, Nathan.
    Explorers for God / Nathan Aaseng : illustrated by Doug Oudekerk.
       p.   cm. — (Family read-aloud collection ; vol. 3)
    Summary: Presents the stories of fifteen men and women whose faith led them
to places around the globe, including Cyril and Methodius, Francis Xavier, Jeanne
Mance, James Marquette, William Penn, Caroline Hershcel, and Jane Franklin.
    ISBN 0-8066-3608-4
    1. Christian biography—Juvenile literature. 2. Explorers—Biography—Juvenile
literature. 3. Missionaries—Biography—Juvenile literature. [1. Christian biography.
2. Missionaries. 3. Explorers.] I. Oudekerk, Douglas, ill. II. Title.
III. Series.
BR1704.A23 1998
270'.092'2—dc21
[B]   98-18815
                                                  CIP
                                                  AC

Manufactured in Hong Kong   AF 9-3608

02   01   00   99   98   1   2   3   4   5   6   7   8   9   10

Contents

FOREWORD

Worlds to Share

WALTER WANGERIN, JR.

ow often I wished I could companion my children through their most difficult experiences—or through their every joy. Too often I learned of the twists of their personal journeys after the fact. I hadn't been there. Moreover, if I had been, I may have been denied full access to—a full understanding of—their hearts and minds in the event.

But there is a way, a blessed way, into the hearts and minds of our children as they journey through life. When the parent reads out loud to the child, the older one becomes the younger one's most intimate companion. They travel together through dangers and delights, through adventures and mysteries, through stories, through genuine experiences—through life itself.

The power of a story well told is to create whole experiences for the child, but controlled experiences with beginnings and middles, and with good endings.

The reward for parents who read such stories to their children is an intimacy that is emotional, spiritual, and real. The walls come down; nothing is hidden between them.

And the benefits to children are legion:

- They are assured that, whatever the experience, they are not alone.

- They are fearless before the circumstances of the story, however frightening or thrilling. And, in consequence, they are prepared to meet similar circumstances in their real life with the boldness and trust that come of experience.

- They, when they laugh heartily, are empowered! For the laughter of children in the face of giants or troubles or evils is their sense of superiority. Their ability to see silliness in danger is their freedom to take spiritual steps above the danger.

- And they are granted a genuine independence, a freedom of choice. For children can choose to hear a fantasy tale as fantasy only, something fun and funny, but not anything you would meet in the real world. And they can listen to stories of distant heroes and heroic deeds as ancient history and nothing to do with their life. Or else they can choose to identify completely with the main character—in which case this fantasy or this ancient story stands for things absolutely real in their own world. Children don't make such choices consciously; they make them in the deep parts of their souls, when they are ready to take the real ride of the story. And the fact that they can and do choose grants them true personhood.

And you, their parent, are there, companioning your child through wonders and terrors, through friendships and wisdom, through experience into experience.

When my father bought a thick book containing all the tales of Hans Christian Andersen and read them to us, he did me a kindness more profound than mere entertainment. He began to weave a world that genuinely acknowledged all the monsters in mine, as well as all the ridiculous situations and silly asides that I as a child found significant. Dad/Andersen was my whispering, laughing, wise companion when I most needed companionship.

Night after night my dad would read a story in his articulate, baritone voice. Gently the voice invited me. Slowly I accepted the invitation and delivered myself to a wonderful world. And as I looked around, I discovered that this world was confident with solutions, and I was a citizen of some authority and reputation. I was no longer alone, no longer helpless.

Dad would sit in a chair beside my bed, one lamp low at his shoulder, his pipe clamped between his teeth and sending the smell of his presence and his affections to me where I lay. Mostly the room, an attic with slanted ceilings, was in darkness. The wind whistled in the eaves.

"Ready?" Dad would say.

We would nod. We would curl tight beneath the covers.

"Once upon a time," Dad would read, sending me straight through the attic walls into the night, onto the wind, for gorgeous, breathtaking flights.

What part of my being could not find affirmation in such an event? My body was present, delighting in its vicarious adventures. All my senses were alert and active, sight and sound and smell and touch. My emotions were given every opportunity—highs so tremendously high, and lows acceptable because Dad was the leader. My mind, my intellect, labored at solutions before the story itself declared them.

And all my affections were granted lovely objects. I could love in that event when my father read to us: I could love characters in the tale; I could love their qualities, their deeds, their struggles; I could love the tale itself—but mostly, I could love my father, whose very voice was his offering of love to me. We were one in this event, one in the reading and in the listening and in the experiencing.

Night after night my father read to us from that thick book. Night after night I lived the adventures that gave order to my turbulent child's experience. The tales gave shape to my waking self, to my instincts, to my faith in God, and to my adulthood yet to come. For I am what I am now, in part, because once I experienced important events within the protected sphere of my father's dear influence.

These events were deep and primal.

But on the page they were merely stories—until my father opened his mouth and read them to me.

The Forbidden Language

CYRIL AND METHODIUS
826–869 • 815–885

*I*t's very difficult to be a Christian if you don't understand the teachings of the church. That was the problem the Moravians faced more than a thousand years ago. The Moravians were the ancestors of the modern group known as the Czechs. They controlled a small empire in southeastern Europe.

In the eighth century, the country converted to Christianity. But Prince Ratislav (RAT-i-slahv), the ruler of Moravia, became frustrated because neither he nor his people understood Latin or Greek—the languages of the church. They spoke a language called Slavonic. After a while, Ratislav asked church leaders to send a missionary who could speak their language.

It so happened that there were two Greek priests, Methodius (Muh-THO-dee-us) and his younger brother Cyril, who knew Slavonic. Methodius had once been governor of a province in which many of the people spoke Slavonic. Cyril was a brilliant scholar who had picked up the language early in his youth.

METHODIUS RUSHED INTO THE LIBRARY waving a letter. "Cyril!" he called, approaching the younger man working at a desk. "I have great news from the church leaders. Read this. You will not believe it!"

Cyril took the letter and studied it. "They're sending us on another mission? So soon? God is indeed smiling on us! You know how I love to explore new places."

"So do I," said Methodius. He studied his brother gravely. "But are you sure you're up to the journey? You are not well. Our last mission to the Caspian Sea took a lot out of you."

"Don't worry about me," insisted Cyril. "This is a wonderful opportunity. Why, we speak Slavonic as well as the Moravians."

"Speak for yourself," said Methodius. "I just know enough to get by; you are the expert."

As the brothers prepared for the trip, Cyril grew concerned. "I have been thinking," he said to Methodius. "The Slavonic language is a spoken language. They have no way of writing it."

Methodius looked puzzled. "Is that a problem?"

"Yes," said Cyril. "You see, the only way they can hear the Word of God is if you or I are there to translate it. But we cannot be everywhere at once," said Cyril. "The Word would spread much more quickly if we could write down a translation the Moravians could read and pass on to others."

"Could they learn to write and read Slavonic using Latin letters?" asked Methodius. "Or perhaps Greek letters?"

"Have you forgotten, the sounds in Slavonic aren't all the same as the sounds spoken in Latin or Greek?"

Methodius shrugged. "Then we must do the best we can with the spoken language. What else can we do?"

Cyril smiled mysteriously. "Perhaps we could invent an alphabet."

"Are you serious?" asked Methodius. "Come now, this language has been around for centuries and no one has been able to put it into written form. Can you create an alphabet out of thin air?"

"Well, not out of air," said Cyril. He showed Methodius a paper filled with strange symbols. "But I think it's worth a try."

Methodius patted him on the back. "It's not enough for you to explore new countries. Now you must explore new alphabets."

When they arrived in Moravia the following year, Cyril's new alphabet was a huge success. Many in Ratislav's court began learning the thirty-eight letters Cyril had created. The emperor and his people rejoiced to see the Bible in words they understood.

As the years passed, the church in Moravia grew stronger and stronger.

"You have done a great work," Methodius said to Cyril. "See how the Word of God is spreading among these people!"

"Yes," said Cyril, thoughtfully. "Still, when I see how eagerly the Moravians devour God's word in their own language, I wonder why we cannot also put the mass (church service) in their language."

"That would be dangerous," warned Methodius. "The mass has always been in Latin. It has been said in Latin for years. The bishops insist it should stay that way."

"But are they right?" asked Cyril.

"Who am I to say?" said Methodius. "But I know we would get in trouble for doing what you suggest. Bishop Wiching (VICK-ing), the German, is already angry with us for translating the Bible into Slavonic. He thinks it cheapens the Holy Word. If we celebrated mass in Slavonic, he would be furious."

"So, who is Bishop Wiching?" Cyril sniffed. "Is he God? No, he is just a man who loves his power and wants to keep it."

"But that is the point," said Methodius. "Wiching does have power. He has been in Moravia much longer than we, and he has powerful friends."

Cyril smiled. "But the emperor is on our side. And even if he were not, should we not do what best serves the glory of God, no matter what the danger?"

Methodius sighed. "You are right of course. Very well. Tomorrow I will say part of the mass in Slavonic, and we shall see what happens."

As Methodius predicted, Bishop Wiching and his followers were outraged. For a long time, however, the brothers ignored them. Many Moravians appreciated being able to understand what was being said in this solemn service.

Cyril never recovered from the illness that struck him on his earlier mission to the Caspian Sea. As he grew weaker, his older brother had to take over most of his official duties. One day after celebrating mass, Methodius found Bishop Wiching waiting for him outside the church.

"How sad," Wiching said, sneering as he handed an official-looking document to Methodius. "I tried to warn you. But you have insisted on perverting the holy mass by using the coarse language of common sinners."

Methodius recognized the seal on the letter as that of the pope, the supreme head of the church. The letter ordered Cyril and Methodius to stop using Slavonic language in the mass. Furthermore, they were to report to Rome to face charges of teaching false ideas.

The trip to Rome was long and hard, especially for Cyril, who was in constant pain from his illness.

"I am sorry I brought us to this point," Cyril said as they approached the hills of Rome. "You were wise to advise caution. Maybe we should have settled for introducing a new alphabet and left the mass alone."

"No," said Methodius. "You were right. The most important thing is helping people to learn about God."

Cyril looked anxiously at his brother. "You know more than I about rules and laws. What will the pope do to us?"

"Don't worry," said Methodius. "You have done your part with the language. Now let me take care of defending us. I have heard that the pope is a good man. I trust he will be fair."

While Methodius went to see the pope, Cyril lay quietly in his bed, worrying. Although he did not tell his brother, Cyril knew that he was dying. Whatever punishment he received would not matter. He would not be around much longer anyway. But he did not want Methodius to suffer.

While Cyril lay praying, Methodius burst into the room. "God be praised! That letter was a hoax. Wiching must have forged it. The pope praised us for our work in Moravia." He sat next to Cyril and chuckled. "I wonder what that fool Wiching was thinking of. How could he believe he would get away with that lie?"

"Wiching may be many things, but he is not a fool," said Cyril thoughtfully. "He must have had some reason for wanting us out of Moravia."

"Well, his plan won't work," Methodius declared. "The pope is sending us back with honors. One of us is to be archbishop of Moravia."

"That will be you," said Cyril. "I will never see Moravia again."

Methodius started to protest. But he saw the truth in Cyril's eyes.

"Do not worry," he said, tears in his eyes. "You have done a great work with your alphabet and with bringing God's word to the common people. As long as God grants me breath, I will carry on what you have started."

Cyril died some weeks later. Despite his grief, Methodius returned to Moravia. As he suspected, Wiching had been busy in his absence. Prince Svatopluk (SVAT-oh-pluck) had overthrown his uncle Rastislav as emperor. Under Wiching's influence, he banned the practice of saying mass in Slavonic. When Methodius defied the order, Svatopluk threw him in prison.

Methodius sat there for two years until the pope finally demanded he be released. As the old priest returned to the church, Wiching was waiting for him.

"I hope you have learned your lesson," he gloated.

Methodius did not answer as he put on his robes. He thought of his last meeting with Cyril and the promise he had made. Then, without another word, he walked to the front of the church. There he began saying the mass—in Slavonic.

*W*hen Methodius died in 885, Svatopluk was determined to destroy everything the old priest had accomplished. He ordered all of Methodius's followers to leave Moravia.

Those followers, however, spread their beliefs to other Slavic countries. Using Cyril's alphabet, they wrote the Word of God for all Slavs to read. While Wiching and Svatopluk had no success getting people to join their version of the faith, Methodius's followers brought the gospel to Russians, Serbs, Bulgarians, and Ukrainians. To this day, those nations continue to use the Cyrillic (suh-RILL-ick) alphabet created by Cyril.

Talk about It

- Cyril and Methodius wanted to make sure Moravian Christians understood not just what they read in the Bible, but what was going on in the church service. Do you always understand what is being said or done in church? When you're in church, notice words that you don't understand and parts of the service that do not make sense to you. After church, ask your parents or the pastor to explain these.

- Some people, like Wiching, don't feel comfortable about changes in the worship service. How do you know when the old, traditional ways are best and when to try something different?

Prayer

God, who watches over all the people of the Earth, help us never to tire of finding ways to tell others about you, so that all your children may know of your power and love. Amen.

A Conqueror's Change of Heart

BARTOLOME DE LAS CASAS
1474–1566

fter hearing tales of his father's adventures sailing with Christopher Columbus, Bartolome de las Casas (Bar-TOLE-uh-may de las CAH-sus) could hardly wait for a chance to explore the New World. What young Spaniard did not long for the chance?! This mystical new territory was bursting with adventures. Rumors spread that the land was full of riches beyond belief, there for the taking.

De las Casas joined a Spanish army expedition charged with conquering Hispaniola (HIS-pan-YOH-la), a large island in the Caribbean Sea, presently divided into the nations of Haiti and the Dominican Republic.

In 1502, the Spanish expedition defeated the native people of Hispaniola (whom the Spanish called "Indians" because Columbus thought he had reached India). Soldiers such as de las Casas were rewarded for their success with large plots of land for farming or mining. They could force the Indians living on this land to work for them without pay.

BARTOLOME DE LAS CASAS pulled off his shiny metal helmet and proudly looked over his new land. "What do you think, Diego?"

Diego nodded. "It is good land. What do you intend to do with it? Mine for gold? Or will you start a farm?"

"Perhaps I will try farming," said de las Casas. "I do not trust gold. You could search for years and not find any."

"Whether farming or mining, we have plenty of Indians to do the work," pointed out Diego. "Good thing, too! I would hate to have to work so hard in this heat."

"True," agreed de las Casas. "I have been thinking, though. Now that we are done fighting the Indians, I would like to try to make Christians out of them. That is what the queen wishes, you know."

"I know how to convert them," said Diego. "Tell them to be Christian or you'll cut their throats. Simple as that."

"I think there is a better way," de las Casas said. "Treat them fairly, with love. Then they'll be more ready to accept Christ."

Diego laughed. "Do not waste your time. These Indians are nothing more than animals. You might as well try to make Christians out of our horses!"

De las Casas's temper flashed. "The Indians are humans like us! It makes me sick to see how some of the soldiers treat them. If I didn't know better, I would say they enjoy killing Indians."

"Whatever you say," sniffed Diego. "If you are so concerned about their souls, maybe you are in the wrong profession. You should be a priest."

There were times in the next few years when de las Casas wondered if Diego was right about the Indians. Although he treated them more kindly than most Spaniards, the Indians did not want to work for him.

"True, working in the stifling heat is no fun," thought de las Casas. "But why can't they see that it is for their own good? The richer I get, the more I can afford to give them." Besides, he was so much kinder than the other Spaniards. Some of them beat their Indians so cruelly he could not stand to be around them.

One day de las Casas returned from a trip to the coast to find only a few Indians working in the fields. "I suppose they have run away again," he said with a sigh.

But when he spoke with the remaining Indians, he learned the terrible news. The absent Indians had not run away; they were dead of smallpox. Many of the remaining Indians were so sick they could barely stand up. De las Casas tried to tend to their illnesses, but he could do nothing. Before long, his farm was virtually empty. With no one left to work the fields, the crops became overgrown with weeds and rotted in the fields.

Diego reported the same problem on his farm. "Some of us are going to the nearby islands to round up more Indians to take the place of the dead," he told de las Casas. "Do you want to join us?"

"Are you sure the government will allow that?" de las Casas asked.

"Spain needs the gold," said Diego. "And I've got a farm and a mine to run. Why should I go bankrupt while there are plenty of Indians around doing nothing?"

Saddened at the thought of forcing more Indians into this miserable existence, de Las Casas shook his head. He began to wonder if he cut out to manage a farm. Maybe there was truth to Diego's teasing about him becoming a priest.

Finally, after hearing yet another report of Indians on a neighboring farm who died from starvation and exhaustion, de las Casas decided he would do it. He would become a priest. Then he could devote his time to proclaiming the Word of God rather than enslaving Indians.

But as he completed his studies for the priesthood, de las Casas ran into financial trouble. With so few Indians left to work his land, he ran short of money. When he heard that Spain was mounting a new conquest, he volunteered to go. Spain had generously rewarded him once. If he helped this new army conquer Cuba, he might get lucky again.

It all seemed so familiar when the army landed on the Cuban shore. The land was filled with Indians—Arawaks and Ciboneys. There were hundreds of thousands of them. But as at Hispaniola, their weapons were no match for Spanish muskets and swords. The Spanish could kill them by the dozens with almost no risk at all.

What was different about this fighting was that de las Casas had changed. He could no longer bear to watch the slaughter of the Indians and the wretched treatment of the prisoners.

When he received another plot of land as a reward for taking part in the expedition, he sat brooding. Should he try again to get the Indians to work under miserable conditions? Maybe they would do better if he tried mining. Maybe he should just stick to his duties as a priest and not worry about the Indians.

No, he realized finally. The whole system was wrong. The Spanish were conquering these people and forcing them to work as slaves under brutal conditions. And he, Bartolome de las Casas, had participated as willingly as the others. He was responsible for mistreating many of God's children. His conscience burned so hot he could hardly sleep at night.

One Sunday morning, de las Casas got up in front of a small congregation. Sweat glistened on his forehead. He knew the people would not like what he had to say. But he refused to stay silent any longer.

"The way we treat the Indians is wrong," he announced. "We have destroyed them as a people. They die by the thousands in our fields or at the hands of our soldiers. And many also die from diseases that we have brought to their land. It is our duty to show them the love of our Lord and Savior, and to bring them peacefully into the faith. That cannot happen as long as we treat them like slaves and animals."

He paused to look over the startled congregation. "Therefore, from this moment," he declared, "I am no longer the master of my farm. I will treat the Indians as I would anyone else. They are free to work for wages, or they may decline to work. I will strive to bring them to Christ as brothers and sisters in the faith."

Several of the most important landowners cornered de las Casas after the service. They were furious. "What do you think you are doing?" one demanded. "How dare you speak against your own country!"

"What do you know of these matters?" another scoffed. "I have heard an older, more experienced priest speak on this same subject. He says that God has condemned these savages for their ungodly ways. It is God's will that we make them work for us."

"Be reasonable," said another, more calmly. "You know yourself how hard it is to survive on these islands so far from Spain. We need the Indians to perform the labor. Our entire New World empire would collapse without them. And God knows these Indians need us. They are so lazy they would starve to death if we did not make them tend our crops."

"How did they manage before we came?" asked de las Casas.

"Enough of your clever words!" said the landowners. "Let your farm go to ruin if that is what you wish. Just don't come running to us when you find yourself broke and starving. You'll never get the rest of us to follow your foolishness."

De las Casas saw that it was hopeless. Nothing he could do would persuade these people. Setting his jaw firmly, he said, "Then I shall go to Spain and speak to the king. If I can persuade him, then you will have to obey."

One of the landowners snarled at him. "You'd better be careful. Anyone who tries to take away our livelihood is our enemy—even if you are a priest. Someday you might wake up to find your house on fire. Maybe you won't wake up at all."

De las Casas knew the landowner was right about what could happen to him if he continued to speak out on behalf of the Indians. His life would be in danger.

"You do what you want," he said. "I will do what I believe is right. I shall be setting sail on the next ship to Spain. And I will not rest until I see justice carried out."

*B*artolome de las Casas sailed to Spain in 1515. He pleaded his case so passionately that the Spanish government formed a commission to oversee the fair treatment of the Indians.

Led by people such as Hernando Cortez, the conqueror of Mexico, the Spanish colonists resisted all change. The Spanish government abandoned the commission.

De las Casas kept prodding the king into passing laws requiring fair treatment of Indians. For a time, he served as a bishop in Guatemala, where he rigidly enforced these laws. The colonists became so angry with him that a mob ransacked his home and tried to kill him. De las Casas barely escaped. But to the end of his ninety-two years, he acted as the conscience of the Spanish New World. His efforts moved Spain to make strides toward treating Indians fairly.

Talk about It

- Why did de las Casas sign up to help conquer Cuba even after he'd been sickened by results of the conquest of Hispaniola? Is the fear of going hungry or losing a job an excuse for taking advantage of other people?

- De las Casas had a very strong conscience that told him how to behave even when it cost him a lot of money. What, exactly, is a conscience? Have you ever had to wrestle with your conscience?

Prayer

We pray today for justice, Lord. Turn our hearts away from our own selfish wants so that we may hear the cries of those who suffer at the hands of their fellow humans, and so that we may work with you for justice. Amen.

The Bell-Ringer vs. the Raiders

FRANCIS XAVIER
1506-1552

 *n the sixteenth century, the king of Portugal sent out an urgent request to the church to send priests into the countries of Asia. He had heard that Portuguese traders living in those lands were falling away from their faith. One of the priests who agreed to go fell ill. At the last minute, Francis Xavier (hah-vee-AIR) agreed to take his place.*

As the ship loaded up to set sail, the king offered Xavier great gifts: the best clothing, food, servants, and whatever else he wanted. Xavier accepted nothing but a robe and a few books. The pope gave Xavier a letter granting him authority over all church officials in Asia. Xavier did not use it.

In fact, Xavier had little interest in anything beyond praising God and helping others. He needed no tools other than his sparkling personality and burning love for Jesus. In 1542, his ship docked at the Portuguese port of Goa in India. From that time on, foreign missions would never be the same.

NO SOONER DID THE BLACK-BEARDED PRIEST stick his head through the doorway than the laughter died. The sailors stopped their card game and looked guilty. The priest rolled his eyes. "You are sailors, not monks," he said, smiling. "Go back to your game." Just as the talk started up again, he shouted, "But . . ."

Again, silence. "Watch your language," warned the priest, a twinkle in his eye.

As the loud play resumed, the priest walked around the room. He made a point of talking to everyone, even the maids and servants. While he did so, a bishop peered suspiciously into the room. Spying the priest, he approached him.

"Ah, Father Francis. I was told you would be here."

When Xavier saw that the visitor was a bishop, he quickly got down on his knees. "Father Francis," said the embarrassed bishop, "it is I who should kneel before you. After all, you are the pope's right-hand man."

"What can I do for you?" Xavier said, rising.

"I came to invite you to stay at my house," said the bishop. "I heard you were living at that filthy hospital among the dying."

"Thank you for the offer," said Xavier. "But my room is better than a palace. My neighbors are some of God's finest people. At any rate, I will not be in Goa much longer."

"Where are you going?" asked the bishop.

"South. Along the coast. I hear the pearl fishers there were baptized some years ago. But they have received no instruction. I have spent weeks memorizing sermons in their language."

"To the Fishery Coast?" asked the bishop. "That is a dangerous journey."

"Dangers are springs of spiritual joy," said Xavier cheerfully.

For weeks, Xavier walked alone through the snake-infested jungle. He slept on the ground, even when rain turned it to a sea of mud. Eating only a small bit of rice each day, he sang hymns that he had made up the night before. At last he came to one of the villages of the Paravas—the pearl divers.

Without stopping to rest, Xavier brought out a small bell and began ringing it. Speaking words that he had memorized, he called out, urging the children to come learn about God. The Paravas did not know what to make of this strange man. The other Europeans they had met showed off their wealth and fine dress. But Xavier came looking much like them. He was barefoot and dirty, and he wore ragged clothes. Curious about this strange man, they sent their children to him. Xavier taught them with rhyming prayers and song so that they could easily remember his words.

Xavier did not learn new languages easily. He relied on phrases he had been taught to say. This system was not perfect, however. Every time Xavier invited the Paravas to celebrate mass with him, they stared at each other in confusion.

Finally, he was able to understand that he had mispronounced the word for mass. The Paravas thought he was inviting them to a "mustache."

Xavier spent his days teaching and baptizing. The Paravas responded eagerly to his kindness and cheerful nature. As his reputation spread, Paravas from other villages gathered to hear him. Sometimes there were so many who wanted to listen that Xavier would climb a tree and shout so all could hear him. Then came the baptisms. After one long day of working with the Paravas, he wrote to his friends back home, "Often my arms are weary from baptizing and I cannot speak another word."

Through prayer and gentle care, Xavier was able to heal some Paravas who were ill. Before long, everyone wanted him to come to their hut to pray for a sick relative. Although he slept only two or three hours a night, Xavier could not get around to everyone. Instead, he taught the people how to pray for their loved ones.

Thousands of miles from his friends, Xavier felt pangs of loneliness. He cut signatures from letters written by his friends. These he pinned on his robe so they would be next to his heart.

One day Xavier watched a group of Paravas head into the ocean in their small boats. They carried only knives and nets. The knives were to fight off sharks. The nets were for collecting oysters that housed precious pearls.

"Grant them success," Xavier prayed. "They are so poor."

Suddenly a messenger raced across the hot sand. "Great Father! Great Father!" he shouted.

"What is the problem?"

The messenger had difficulty making himself understood. At last the problem became clear: The Bandagas had come!

The Bandagas were fierce warriors from the north. Mounted on horses sold to them by the Portuguese, they had raided a neighboring village.

Xavier hurried as fast as he could through the thick jungle. When he arrived at the village hours later, he found a horrifying sight. The village had been burned. Several villagers lay dead. Others had been carried off into slavery.

Worse yet, the fierce Bandagas had promised they would return. They planned to destroy all the Paravas' villages.

Xavier was furious when he learned that his own countrymen had supplied the Bandagas with horses and weapons for the raid. He sent letters to government officials asking them to put a stop to such wicked trading.

But he knew nothing would be done about that for a long time. Meanwhile, the Paravas were in grave danger from the brutal raiders. For the next few months, Xavier worked himself to a frenzy.

Much of his time was spent organizing efforts to bring food to those whose villages had been destroyed. The Paravas did not have weapons or training to defeat men on horseback. But there were some things they could do. Xavier worked alongside the people to build a series of large trenches around the villages. They also planted rows of thick, tangled hedges. These would slow down the horses so the Paravas would have a chance to escape when the Bandagas attacked.

Xavier walked from village to village helping the Paravas prepare their defenses. One day he stood alone on the dirt trail, eating his noon meal of toasted rice grains. He heard what sounded like thunder, yet the sky was blue and cloudless.

Grimly, Xavier realized what was happening. The thunder was horses' hooves of the Bandagas. The raiders were coming again! He would have to move quickly if he wanted to hide.

But Xavier did not move.

A minute later, the Bandagas charged around the bend. The snorting white horses headed straight for Xavier, ready to trample him.

Xavier refused to move. He reached inside his cloak and pulled out his crucifix. Planting himself firmly in the path, he held the crucifix in front of him. When the horsemen were nearly on top of him, their leader wheeled to a halt. Through a cloud of dust, he glared at the priest.

"In the name of God, I ask you to turn around and leave these people in peace," Xavier said firmly.

An interpreter relayed the message to the startled Bandagas captain. The captain laughed. "You cannot stop us. Step aside before we kill you!"

"I will not step aside," Xavier cooly replied. "You will not harm these people."

The captain stared at him. He wondered about the courage of this strange man and about the cross the man held in front of him. "You are a brave—or very foolish man," he said to Xavier. "But . . . one man against an army? This is madness!"

"Breaking the laws of God by murdering innocent people is madness," answered the priest. "You are the one who should be afraid."

The captain stared at him for a long while, unsure of what to do. He had never seen anyone show such courage. Finally, he waved his arm in the direction they had come. Xavier watched them leave. Then with a deep sigh of thanks, he continued on his way, making up a new hymn as he went.

*F*rancis Xavier helped arrange a treaty that stopped the Bandagas' raids. The Paravas were convinced they owed their survival to the cheerful, tireless man in the ragged robes. From that time onward, the Paravas have remained unshakable in the faith that Xavier taught them.

Francis Xavier continued his daring quest to bring the good news of Jesus to the ends of the earth. He was one of the first Europeans to set foot in the empire of Japan. Always eager for new adventures, he died of illness while attempting to gain entrance into the mysterious land of China. He is remembered as one of the most beloved and successful missionaries of all time.

Talk about It

- Standing up—all alone—to the Bandagas was a remarkably brave thing to do. Do you think Xavier knew that the Bandagas would turn around and leave him in peace? If not, why would he do such a thing? What lesson can you learn from this about what to do when you feel frightened?

- Why do you think Xavier refused all the offers of gifts and power? Did this attitude have anything to do with his great success as a missionary?

Prayer

Read Psalm 43, verses 1–3, aloud. Then, as a family, pray for the courage to stand up for what is right.

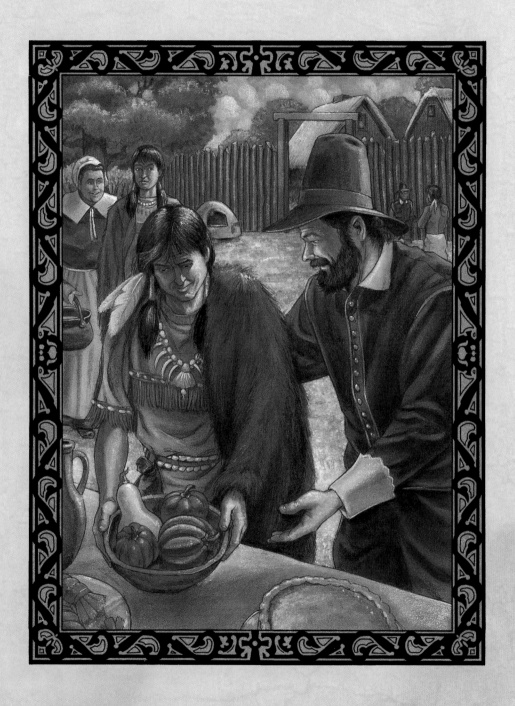

Thank You!

WILLIAM BRADFORD
1590–1657

 *ometimes you know exactly where you are going, and sometimes you just go where the wind blows you. The group that we have come to know as the Pilgrims missed their mark by several hundred miles. Strong winds blew their ship, the* Mayflower, *far north of their intended target.*

The Pilgrims were people who disagreed with the policies of the official Church of England. They wanted their church to be like the early Christian communities where everyone took part in decisions and worked together for the good of the group. They did not want to take orders from high church officials. Unfortunately for them, the king was the leader of the Church of England. Anyone who opposed the official church, therefore, opposed the king. Opposing the king was treason.

The Pilgrims were persecuted so badly for their beliefs that they fled to Holland. There they enjoyed freedom to worship as they pleased. But most were farmers who now had no land and could not make a living. In September of 1620, they sailed to the New World colony of Virginia and ended up far north—off the coast of Massachusetts.

WILLIAM BRADFORD COULD SEE that they had not chosen the best time to sail into the New World. A cold north wind blew off the land and swept over the harbor where they had docked. And if the weather followed the same pattern as in Europe, winter was only beginning.

"I am afraid this is not Virginia," said the group's leader.

Like most of the Pilgrims, Bradford did not care where they were. After a miserable two-month voyage on a small ship crammed with 102 passengers, he just wanted to get onto solid land. Any land.

The Pilgrims finally decided to send scouts to see if any land near this bay was suitable for building a settlement.

"Can we not all go to shore?" pleaded Dorothy Bradford to her husband. "I hate this ship. The smell is so bad I can never keep any food down."

"You must bear it a short while longer," said William. "Remember the stories of the Indians? There may be many of them in this area. The ship is the only safe place for now."

"Please hurry, then!" she cried. "Oh, there are many times I wish we had never come. I miss our little son terribly."

William patted her hand. "We will send for our son as soon as we are settled in this new place."

Although William tried to speed up the search, the scouts could not agree on the best spot for a settlement. One of the men suggested they look at a deserted Indian village.

"Fine. Let us scout it out at once!" said Bradford.

"Are you mad?" others laughed. "In this snowstorm?"

Bradford knew that Dorothy and the other women were being driven near madness by being cooped up on the ship. The group needed to decide on a site—fast! He and a few others slogged through snow deeper than they had ever seen. The abandoned village appeared to be an ideal location.

At last! Bradford thought as they hurried back to the ship. Now they could end this waiting and push on with their dream.

But when Bradford reached the *Mayflower*, he saw pity and sadness in the faces that greeted him.

"What is it?" he demanded. Dorothy! He looked around frantically to find his wife. Where was she?

"There was no warning," he was told. "The first thing we heard was the splash. We do not know how she fell from the deck. But we could not save her."

Suddenly Bradford was alone, his son thousands of miles across the ocean, his wife gone. Had she slipped and fallen into the water, or had she jumped—driven by the hardships into which he had led her?

But there was no going back now, even if he wanted to. Bravely, Bradford worked to establish the new colony in spite of his grief. Not only did he build a small wood and mud hut for himself, but he helped others to get theirs up before they froze in the winter snow.

Bradford had known the first year would be a challenge. But neither he nor any of the rest was prepared for the nightmare of that first winter. Never had the Pilgrims felt such a stinging cold. Never had they tromped through such deep snow. Never had a winter lasted so long.

The settlement ran low on food. Disease struck even more savagely than the north wind. One by one Bradford's friends died in their beds. On many nights, Bradford and the few others who could lift a shovel trudged out into the snow to bury the latest victim. They did not dare do the job during the day for fear the Indians would see them. If the Indians knew how few Pilgrims were left, they might attack the settlement.

By the time the snow melted, the community was in deep trouble. Only four of the fourteen married women who had come ashore still survived. Half the men were gone, including all the leaders. They were now down to the thirty-one-year-old William Bradford as their chosen governor. The wise thing would have been to admit failure and sail back to England.

But Bradford and the others refused to give up the dream of a community where they could worship as they pleased. They set about tasks to prepare for the next winter. Everyone collected and chopped wood from the forest, built and repaired dwellings, thatched roofs, and planted and tended crops.

Even though they were working themselves to the bone, Bradford worried about the future. Would they have enough food to see them through the next winter? Would the Indians attack them now that they were few and weak?

Fortunately, Bradford found help from the very people they feared. Seeing that the Pilgrims posed no threat to them, some of the Indians befriended the new arrivals.

One Indian in particular, named Squanto, showed them many tricks of survival in this new land. He pointed out which roots and berries were good to eat and how to store them. He introduced them to a new, fast-growing crop called maize (corn), and taught them the technique of planting dead fish with the seeds to act as fertilizer.

When autumn came, Bradford looked over the stocks of food and firewood, and the solid houses. If they could somehow avoid another bout of disease, they were set for the winter.

"What a change!" he thought. Less than a year ago, the place seemed doomed. The new world had seemed so stingy and brutal and full of heartbreak and death. He still ached at the thought of Dorothy and he longed to see his son. How the boy must be growing!

But now he saw that this new world was one of plenty. God had provided everything they would need for the coming winter. The Pilgrims were living their dream, free to worship as they saw fit.

One day Bradford approached the settlers with a proposal. "God has blessed us richly," he said. Most of the Pilgrims agreed with him. Perhaps some, remembering the agonies of the past winter and the loss of so many loved ones, stayed silent.

"We must do something to thank God for seeing us through these hardships and providing us with so much for the coming winter," he said.

"What do you have in mind?"

"A feast. A celebration," Bradford said.

"How can we feast and celebrate soon after going through so much pain?" one asked.

"When I lived in Leyden, Holland," Bradford explained, "they had a holiday every year—a special day of thanksgiving. It seems that about fifty years ago the Spanish had attacked and surrounded the city. Thousands of people were killed before the Spanish finally were driven off. But the people celebrated this feast of thanksgiving every year to thank God for delivering them. I think we have lived through a similar trial. Let us make a special day to thank God for delivering us from the horrors of last winter and for providing for us this harvest season."

Bradford spoke so persuasively that the Pilgrims agreed. They set aside one day for nothing but feasting and thanksgiving. Everyone would eat together and afterward join in songs and games and laughter.

Someone came up with the daring idea of inviting the Indians to the feast as well. "After all, we would not have all this food if they had not helped us," they said.

Indians and Pilgrims sharing together in a great feast? Would it work? Bradford sent the invitation to Massasoit (ma-suh-SOYT), chief of the Wampanoag (wahm-puh-NOH-ag) Indians who had been such good neighbors.

On the day of the feast, the Pilgrims filled their tables with wild turkey, shellfish, and a kind of pudding made from corn.

"Do we have enough?" they asked. "How many Indians are coming? What if there are too many for us to feed?"

They did not have to worry. When Massasoit and ninety of his tribe appeared from out of the woods, they were carrying five deer to share with the settlers. The feast went on all day, with Indians joining in the songs and the games. As Bradford watched it all, he thought back to the dark nights of the previous winter. They had been afraid to move far beyond sight of their houses for fear of the Indians. They had lain at night with their stomachs growling from hunger. Who ever would have predicted the joyful scene that played before him now?

Bradford closed his eyes and repeated over and over. "Thank you, Lord God. Thank you."

In 1863, the United States was locked in the agony of a terrible civil war. At that time, President Abraham Lincoln thought back to the courage and optimism of Bradford and the Pilgrims. He asked the nation to remember in this time of crisis the many blessings that God had provided. By presidential order, he declared the feast of Thanksgiving a national holiday, which we celebrate to this day.

Talk about It

- Considering all he had lost, did Bradford really have a lot to be thankful for? What makes people like him—and us—feel thankful? What keeps us from feeling thankful?

- Bradford did more than just say thanks to God. He declared a feast and shared it with the Indians. What are some special ways we can thank God other than in prayer? Why is giving thanks far more important to us than it is to God?

Prayer

Thank you, Lord, for this precious day. We thank you for all those things we need to live, things we often take for granted: food, shelter, sunshine, a warm bed, schools, friends, and family. Amen.

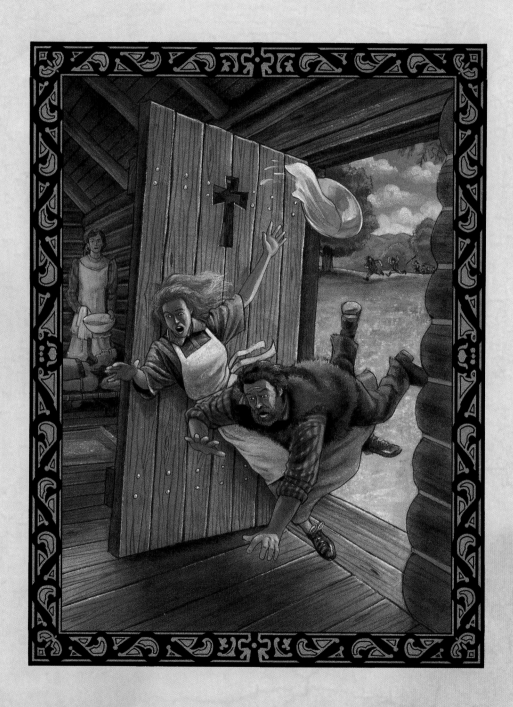

Hospital in the Wilderness

JEANNE MANCE
1606–1673

 hen Jeanne (ZHAHN) Mance was thirteen, she heard tales of her uncle who had gone to New France (now Eastern Canada) to bring Christianity to the Indians. The stories of an endless forest filled with animals and fast-flowing rivers and strange people sounded like a fairy tale come true. But she realized that her chances of ever seeing this wilderness were slim. Women at that time were not allowed to explore. The only way they could get to a place like New France was if a husband brought his wife to help start a settlement. Mance didn't want to get married; she felt called to dedicate her life to God.

More than twenty years later, though, opportunity fell into Mance's lap. A wealthy widow wanted to build a hospital for a new settlement in New France. She asked Mance to take charge of the hospital. Mance gathered her courage and, in June of 1641, sailed across the ocean to Quebec, the major settlement in New France. Over the furious objections of Governor Montagny (mohn-TAYH-nee), she and forty-five settlers headed into the western wilderness in May of the following year.

"SO THIS IS THE PLACE I have heard so much about!" exclaimed Mance. There was no mistaking the place the explorers called Montreal. Here was the large island in the middle of the river. Over to the north stood the towering Mount Royale from which the place took its name.

"Do you need help pitching your tent?" asked Maisonneuve (may-zoh-NOOV), leader of the settlers. He was aware that Mance had nearly died from the bad food and water on the stormy ocean voyage. She still seemed as though a strong wind would blow her away.

"I am fine. You worry about yourself," said Mance.

"Worry is right," remarked Maisonneuve, glancing nervously at the thick forests. "You heard what the governor said about the Iroquois. No one is safe from those Indians these days. I shall feel better once we have built a fort."

The Iroquois, however, did not appear that summer or fall. Undisturbed, the settlers were able to finish building their permanent shelters just in time for winter. They harvested a crop that would help them get through until spring.

For the first year, Jeanne Mance spent most of her time cooking, tending gardens, doing chores, and learning the Indians' languages. Every once in a while she would treat a wounded Huron Indian or care for a sick settler.

"Are you sure you know what you are doing?" teased one settler after recovering from a flu. "I hear you're not a trained nurse."

"I cared for ten brothers and sisters after my parents died," Mance answered. "That is more practice than many nurses get."

One day one of the Frenchmen working the fields saw Indians coming out of the woods. "Uh-oh!" he said warily. "Look who's coming."

"Relax," said another. "They are Hurons. Probably here to trade with us."

As the men went back to their hoeing, shrill cries broke out from the woods on both sides. Dozens of other Indians dashed out of the woods brandishing weapons.

"Iroquois ambush! Run!"

The warlike Iroquois had tracked the Hurons, who were their enemies, and meant to wipe them out. Both Hurons and French settlers raced frantically for the fort. Some did not make it. Many others arrived clutching painful wounds. Suddenly Mance found herself overwhelmed by patients with ghastly injuries. But she steadied herself and performed her job well.

"We are lucky," said Maisonneuve as he watched her wash a deep knife wound. "How many wilderness outposts have their own nurse?"

"We must have more than a nurse," said Mance. "It's time to get that hospital built."

"Is that wise?" asked Maisonneuve. "There are too few of us yet to need a hospital. You know the dangers we face. How can we spare the time and effort on a building we do not yet need?"

"I came here to run a hospital," said Mance firmly. "That is what I plan to do."

Under her direction, the settlers built a hospital about ten minutes' walk from the fort. Mance called it the Hotel Dieu (oh-tel D'YEW)—the Hotel of God.

"There's your hospital," said Maisonneuve when the building was complete. "Now leave it be except for emergencies. We do not want you out here away from the fort without protection. The Iroquois have been stepping up their attacks."

"What good is a hospital without a nurse?" asked Mance. Despite Maisonneuve's pleas, she went to the hospital every day.

The Iroquois remained on the rampage. Their attacks brought a steady stream of slashed and bleeding Hurons to the remarkable nurse of the wilderness. Several families, too, had joined the Montreal settlement, bringing their children with them. A few of these had fallen victim to Iroquois attacks. In addition to her nursing duties, Mance took in the orphans and cared for them.

One afternoon in May of 1652, a warm sun shone on the Montreal settlement. Working in the hospital, Mance decided to take advantage of the pleasant spring weather. She propped open the heavy wooden door so she could enjoy the breezes.

All at once she heard shouts from outside. As she went to look out the door, LeMoyne, one of the settlers, bowled her over as he dashed inside. His eyes were filled with terror.

Mance heard a "thump" in the wood just above her head. A hatchet blade quivered, buried deep in the door. As she picked herself off the floor, Mance glanced out and saw two settlers running for their lives. More than two dozen Iroquois raced after them; several were only a few yards behind.

"Run, Denis! Run, Charles!" she shrieked. Charles cried out in pain as something struck him in the back. Mance feared that the two wouldn't make it. But both dove through the open door. Mance looked right into the face of one of the Iroquois just before she and LeMoyne slammed the door shut.

They bolted the door and waited anxiously for an attack. But when evening came, all was quiet. The Iroquois had left.

"That does it!" said LeMoyne. "Your door was wide open. If the Iroquois had not run into us first, and had we not happened to run this way, they would have walked right in here."

"Yes, from now on you stay in the fort and work here only with a guard," said Denis.

Shaken by the close call, Mance reluctantly agreed.

As the Iroquois attacks continued, even the fort could not keep the settlers safe. By the end of the year, thirty of the seventy French adventurers had fallen to Iroquois braves.

Maisonneuve was forced to call a meeting. When he looked at the remaining settlers, he saw fear, sadness, and hopelessness in their eyes. "I guess the governor was right," he said at last. "This wilderness is simply too dangerous, especially for those with families. Perhaps we must leave Montreal."

"I can understand if you all wish to leave," said Mance firmly. "But my job is to run the hospital here in Montreal. If there are those who would like to stay, there is something I can do for you. People in France have been generous in their gifts to the hospital. Take some of my funds to hire a company of soldiers. Then we shall be safe."

Maisonneuve shook his head. "That money was given for a hospital, not for soldiers. We cannot take it."

"There will be no hospital without a settlement," said Mance. "And there will be no settlement without protection. So you see, the money is going toward the work of the hospital. Go now and get the soldiers."

"But I am the leader; I cannot abandon you!" cried Maisonneuve. "Traveling back to France and hiring soldiers will take time. What will you do in the meantime?"

Mance smiled. "Remember I once took care of ten children when I was but a child myself. We will manage."

Cheered by Mance's determination, most of the settlers stayed.

Maisonneuve headed east, anxiety gnawing at the pit of his stomach. He looked back one last time at the fort. What would he find when he returned? If the Iroquois did not overwhelm them all, the alternative was probably worse. The settlers would be so busy guarding each other from attack that they would be unable to tend the crops. They would starve before the next winter was over.

When he returned to France, one maddening delay after another thwarted his efforts. By the time he got the soldiers together and arranged passage back to New France, a year had passed.

"Is there any point in going back?" Maisonneuve wondered. Almost two years after leaving Jeanne Mance and the others to fend for themselves, he drew near Montreal.

There was the fort! There were settlers in the field. They were hungry and ragged—but they were alive. Best of all, he found Mance tidying up in the hospital.

"I did not expect to find you alive," said Maisonneuve as he hugged her.

"Of course, I am alive. I have a hospital to run." Then, more seriously, she added, "We prayed for strength. God gave it to us."

*J*eanne Mance's courage and determination won admirers throughout New France. More than forty babies born in the early years of the French colony were named after her. The settlement that she helped hold together eventually became one of the largest cities in Canada.

Talk about It

- What was behind Jeanne Mance's fierce determination to keep her little hospital going? Mance could be described as a very stubborn person. In what ways can stubbornness be good? In what ways can it be a problem?

- When Mance was young and living in France, life in New France seemed wonderfully romantic to her—"a fairy tale come true." How do you think she felt about New France several years after she arrived there? What might have changed her attitude and feelings? Tell about a time when your hopes and dreams about a place, a job, a person didn't match your actual experience with that place, job, or person. How do we rebuild our enthusiasm and good spirits when this happens?

Prayer

God in heaven, help us be faithful in all we do. Give us strength to continue when the going seems hopeless. Rebuild our spirit, courage, and joy in those times. And help the light of our spirit and our faith in you to shine so brightly that we inspire others to continue their work to the glory of your name. Amen.

Mystery of the Great River

JACQUES MARQUETTE
1637–1675

ivers are an explorer's best friend. You can't easily get lost on them because rivers have a starting point and an ending point. Floating on water takes much less effort than hiking through bogs, thick woods, and steep mountains. That is why European explorers were so curious about the majestic waterway the Indians called "The Father of Waters." Did this mighty river, which we know as the Mississippi, flow south to the Gulf of Mexico? Or did it flow west to the Pacific Ocean? If it veered west, it could provide the water passage to the Pacific that explorers had been seeking for many years. If it flowed south, it could provide an important waterway from the Great Lakes to the Gulf of Mexico.

The French, who claimed some of the land through which the Mississippi flowed, sent fur trader Louis Jolliet (LOO-ee zhohl-YAY) to find out. In late 1672, Jolliet began to put together one of the smallest and most unusual exploration parties ever to probe the American wilderness. As the last stop before heading out, he visited the new mission of St. Ignace in northern Michigan.

FATHER JACQUES (ZHAHK) MARQUETTE grew envious as he listened to his friend Jolliet talk about his new assignment. Imagine being the first European to sail this great river to its end! Since his arrival in America six years ago, Marquette had been itching to explore. But he had been assigned other duties—to minister to Indians of the western Great Lakes.

"Well, I wish you luck," Marquette said wistfully.

"I am expecting more than wishes from you," said Jolliet. There was a twinkle in his eye. "I need someone with me who speaks Indian languages. I understand you are an expert."

Marquette was flustered for a moment. "What? You mean you are asking me to come with you? But are you certain? The Indians who dwell along the Mississippi probably do not speak the same language as those around here."

"Nonetheless, they are more likely to understand you than me," said Jolliet. "So, are you coming?"

Marquette could hardly believe his good fortune. How many priests got such a chance? Of course he would come.

With barely a thought of the dangers ahead, he set out with Jolliet and five companions in May 1773. Paddling two birchbark canoes, they wound their way down the Fox and Wisconsin Rivers toward the Mississippi. Along the way, they stopped at a camp of Illinois Indians, who gave them a warm welcome.

The Illinois were impressed by the courage of these seven men who were sailing into the unknown with no warriors to protect them. The chief gave the travelers a calumet—a kind of pipe for smoking.

"This is a symbol of peace," said the chief, placing the decorated pipe in Marquette's hand. "Perhaps it will help you make peace with the tribes you meet."

Marquette thanked him for the gift, and the adventurers continued their voyage. They reached the Mississippi and began heading south.

Day after day they paddled along the great river. The trip was not always exciting. They baked in the heat of the sun, which grew hotter as they moved south. But each day brought fascinating sights and sounds. The explorers gazed in wonder at the spectacular steep bluffs that bordered the river. They watched strange birds and listened to the bellowing of a herd of bison.

Always the river carried them south. The explorers began to suspect that the great river was carrying them toward the Gulf of Mexico, not the Pacific Ocean.

After many days of travel, the seven paddled near a thickly wooded shore. The summer heat was stifling. Marquette's eyes glazed over as they glided by huge cottonwood trees.

All at once, piercing shouts rose from the bank. Marquette saw a large Indian village on a flat clearing between stands of trees. Dozens of angry young men brandishing clubs, hatchets, and bows and arrows ran to the edge of the river.

Jolliet picked up his musket and cradled it in his hands. All the other Frenchmen except Marquette did the same.

A few warriors charged into the river and waded toward the French canoes. Quickly, the Frenchmen steered away from the shore. Then Marquette heard a splash. Several groups of Indians were pushing canoes into the water. Shouting fiercely, they paddled toward the explorers.

"Pull hard, men!" shouted Jolliet. "We must get away from here!" But the Indians split up—some paddled upriver, some downstream. One canoe steered far out into the channel to keep the Frenchmen from escaping to the far shore.

"We shall have to fight our way out of this," Jolliet cried. "Quickly, before we get boxed in. Muskets ready!"

"No!" called Marquette. He hated fighting and killing. His mission was to bring Christ's peace and love to all people. He would continue do so, regardless of the risk. Struggling to keep from swamping the canoe, Marquette rose to his feet. He stood tall in the canoe and lifted the Illinois calumet high over his head. Then he held it out toward the Indians.

The peace symbol, however, meant nothing to the attackers. They whooped and shouted all the louder. While Jolliet's men fingered the triggers of their muskets, the Indian canoe farthest out in the river pulled closer. It crowded them and began forcing them toward shore.

"We cannot hold off any longer!" Jolliet insisted. "If they get us near the shore, we won't have a chance."

"They will overwhelm us at any rate if we try to fight," said Marquette. "There are too many of them." Gazing steadily at the approaching canoes, he continued to hold out the pipe.

The warriors paid no attention. One man hurled his club. Marquette flinched as it sailed just past his shoulder. Braves in several canoes fitted arrows to their bows.

"Shoot now before it's too late!" shouted one of the Frenchmen.

"Not yet!" pleaded Marquette, still holding out his pipe. He hoped his attempt at peace had not already doomed his companions. By his actions, he had let the Indians come so close that the muskets would be of little use.

The attackers in the nearest canoe reached out to grab Marquette's canoe. The priest nearly lost his balance.

Jolliet lifted his musket and aimed. "We have no choice . . ." he started.

He was interrupted by two very different shouts from the bank. These were older voices—strong voices that carried across the water over the shouts of the young warriors.

The Indians in the canoes looked back at the two elders on the shore. After a few more words from the older men, the attacking braves looked suspiciously at the calumet. Then, still scowling, they put away their weapons.

The older Indians beckoned the visitors to the shore.

"Do you suppose this is some trick?" asked one of the explorers. Marquette shook his head. He saw no danger in the eyes of the elders.

"That was a very near thing," the explorers said.

"Indeed it was," replied Jolliet. "Had we fired at them, who knows what might have happened!"

"I believe they were as frightened of us as we were of them," said Marquette. "We only needed to let them know we come as friends. Fortunately, the older ones understood the meaning of the calumet."

One of the Indians climbed aboard Marquette's canoe as it headed for shore. He poked at the canoe with his knife and laughed as his blade went right through it. Peeling a bit of the bark from the canoe, he called to his mates.

"See, their canoes are made of solid wood," said Jolliet. "They have never seen a birch canoe. I imagine everything about us is strange. No wonder they acted as they did."

The Indians welcomed them and took them to their main camp down the river. Communicating with their hosts was difficult, but Marquette found a few who understood a bit of the Huron language. From these he learned that these people called themselves the Quapaw.

When Marquette told of their mission to follow the Mississippi to its end, the Quapaw frowned and raised their voices.

"What is the problem?" Jolliet said nervously. "You did not offend them, did you?"

Marquette struggled to understand the Quapaws' speech. After a long time, interrupted by questions, he understood.

"They say that we should not go any farther," he explained. "A warlike tribe lives just to the south. Apparently, they are armed with muskets."

"Muskets? How can that be? Where did they get muskets?" demanded the explorers.

"Could it be that they trade with the Spanish?" said Jolliet. Spanish explorers had claimed most of the region near the Gulf of Mexico for their country. They had established some ports and settlements. France and Spain were currently enemies.

The Quapaw described white men to the south who must certainly have been the Spanish.

"Then we must be near the Gulf of Mexico," said Jolliet. "The Mississippi flows into it then, does it not?"

Marquette put the question to the Quapaw. They told him that ten days' travel along the river would take them to the sea.

Jolliet thought for a while and then said, "That answers the riddle we were sent to solve. I see no point in continuing farther. We are not strong enough to challenge the Spanish nor Indians with guns. Thanks to Father Marquette's cool head and the calumet, we were warned in time to avoid disaster. Let us turn back toward home."

Talk about It

- These explorers narrowly avoided a disaster that arose because of fear and misunderstanding. What was there about Father Marquette that helped him turn the situation around? If his tactic hadn't worked—if the explorers had all been killed—would Marquette have been wrong? What are ways you can prevent misunderstandings from turning into fights?

Prayer

Pray the following prayer, attributed to Saint Francis of Assisi. Memorize the first two lines so you can pray them again.

> *Lord, make me an instrument of your peace.*
> *Where there is hatred, let me sow love;*
> *where there is injury, pardon;*
> *where there is discord, union;*
> *where there is doubt, faith;*
> *where there is despair, hope;*
> *where there is darkness, light;*
> *where there is sadness, joy.*
> *Grant that I may not so much seek*
> *to be consoled as to console;*
> *to be understood as to understand;*
> *to be loved as to love.*
> *For it is in giving that we receive;*
> *it is in pardoning that we are pardoned; and*
> *it is in dying that we are born to eternal life.*

Let Freedom Ring

WILLIAM PENN
1644-1718

illiam Penn knew he was going to get in huge trouble at home. The Penns were Cavaliers—wealthy, upper-class supporters of the king. Penn's father was an important admiral in the British navy. If there was one group their family wanted nothing to do with, it was the Society of Friends. The Friends refused to fight, even in the service of the king. They also believed all people were equal, and so they refused to show proper respect to the king and other nobles. The Penns thought of them as traitors who should be locked up.

But William Penn was a headstrong young man. He had already been thrown out of Oxford University for criticizing the Church of England. While visiting Ireland on business for his father in 1667, he attended meetings of the Friends. Penn was so moved by their silent, prayerful services that he joined them.

Embarrassed by his son's actions, Penn's father ordered William to move out of the house. Dressed in his fine clothes and wig, Penn attracted a great deal of attention for joining the lowly, outcast Friends. Authorities were eager to make an example of this man who had betrayed his own class.

WILLIAM PENN WAS FUMING! How dare this grubby soldier barge into a prayer service of the Friends and try to pick a fight! When the oaf stuck his leering, whiskery chin into the face of a young woman who sat in silent prayer, Penn's temper blew.

With one hand he picked up the soldier by the collar. With the other he grabbed the man by the seat of his pants and marched him toward the door. As Penn started to toss the soldier down the stairs, the Friends surrounded him.

"William, please! Violence is not our way."

Penn wanted desperately to give the man the thrashing he deserved. But the Friends believed God hated violence of any kind. Reluctantly, he let the man go. The soldier immediately ran to the authorities. Before long, law officers arrived and arrested Penn and eighteen others for plotting against the government—the usual charge against Friends.

When the judge saw the expensively dressed Penn among the criminals, he immediately ordered him released. "You fools!" he scolded the officers. "That man obviously is not one of them."

"Yes, I am," Penn insisted. Finally, the baffled judge sent him off to prison. It was the first of several brief jail sentences that Penn served over the next few years. Each stay made him more determined to fight for the rights of people to worship God as they saw fit.

In 1670, the English government cracked down even harder on religious groups that did not obey the Church of England. As usual, the Friends were one of their primary targets.

Penn decided to fight for his beliefs no matter the cost. On August 14, 1670, he marched to the doors of a meeting hall that had been boarded up and began to speak to the Friends assembled outside. Curious about the Cavalier who was spouting radical beliefs, a large crowd gathered. This was exactly what the Lord Mayor of London had hoped would happen.

Under the new laws, the mayor believed Penn's actions would land the traitor in jail for a long time. He had Penn and his friend, William Mead, arrested and charged them with being in contempt of the king and with disturbing the peace.

"How do you plead?" asked the mayor when Penn stood before him in the courtroom.

"I should like to see a copy of the charges so I may know how to plead," Penn answered.

The mayor refused to read the charges. Smugly, he asked Penn to remove his hat as a sign of respect for the court. He knew that the Friends removed their hats for no one.

"We show respect in other ways—not by removing our hats," William replied.

"I shall fine you for contempt of court," snarled the mayor.

Seeing that they could expect no fairness from the mayor, Penn asked for a jury trial on the charges, as was his right. The mayor had to grant the request, but he remained the presiding judge at the trial.

When the mayor called the court to order, the government brought forth three witnesses.

"Did you see this man preaching before a large and unruly crowd?" asked the prosecutor, pointing at Penn.

All three said they had.

The mayor smiled at the jury. "There you have it. The evidence against him is overwhelming."

"But speaking is not a crime," argued Penn. "We were trying to worship. So was that my crime? Attempting to worship God?"

"No! You are charged with unlawful assembly against the king!" the mayor snapped.

"Where is the law that says I cannot worship God?" demanded Penn. "Please read it to me."

The mayor was being so unfair that Penn had to struggle to keep his temper. "As an Englishman, I have the right to know what crime I am charged with," he said. "If you will not read me the law that says I cannot worship God, then you are in the wrong. You prove that you have no interest in justice."

"That does it!" fumed the mayor. "Put him away where he cannot disrupt the proceedings." The jailers seized Penn and locked him in a small closet in a corner of a courtroom.

Scrunched down in the tiny closet, Penn tried to focus on God and block out hateful thoughts. But it was so exasperating. He had hoped to plead his case to the jury. He thought he could persuade them that sincere people should be allowed to worship God in peace. But the mayor was not giving him a chance!

Once again, he heard the muffled voice of the prosecutor reminding the court that three witness had heard Penn preaching to an unruly crowd.

"You have before you the facts," the mayor said to the jury. "Go now and do your duty."

Penn moaned in despair. Given the mayor's orders, the jury would surely find him guilty. His temper erupted again.

"The jury cannot decide anything until I have had a chance to defend myself! This is not legal!" he shouted through a slit in the closet.

This time the jailer hauled Penn away to a prison.

"You can wait here until the jury reaches a verdict," said the jailer. "It shouldn't be long."

Penn sat in silent prayer while he waited. A little while later, the jailer returned and led Penn back to the courtroom.

Penn took one look at the mayor's gloating face and then at the faces of the jurors. Did he see a glimmer of hope in one juror's eyes?

"How do you find the defendant?" asked the mayor.

"Guilty," said the jury foreman. Penn slumped in dejection. He was not looking forward to prison. He liked his wealth and comforts. But what infuriated him was the unfairness of it all.

The foreman continued. "We find the defendant guilty of speaking on Gracious Street."

"You mean guilty of unlawful assembly," said the mayor.

"No," said the foreman. "He is guilty of speaking to a crowd. That is all."

Penn perked up. What was the jury doing? Were they actually thinking of letting him go free despite the mayor's wishes?

"He is not charged with speaking to a crowd," said the mayor. "His crime is leading an unlawful assembly. Now go back in that room and come out with a proper verdict."

The jury filed out. Penn returned to his filthy cell. But now he was hopeful. He sensed that the jury wanted to allow freedom of worship. "Give them the courage to stand up for their beliefs," he prayed.

Back they came into the courtroom for the verdict. The foreman stared hard at the mayor. "We find William Penn guilty of speaking," he said.

"To an unlawful assembly," hissed the mayor.

"No!" replied the foreman.

"I shall lock you up! I shall fine you! I shall starve you until you give the correct verdict!" warned the mayor.

Penn interrupted. "You are Englishmen," he said to the jury. "Your decision is law. Hold on to your rights."

The mayor locked up the jury for two more nights. The jury and Penn then returned to the courtroom a third time.

"Have you come to your senses and changed your verdict?" demanded the mayor.

"Yes, we have," answered the foreman.

Penn looked at the floor and shook his head. How could he blame the jurors? They wanted to go back to their homes and families. The mayor was forcing them to reach the verdict he wanted. Fighting for people's freedom to worship God according to their own beliefs was going to be a long, hard fight.

The foreman set his jaw and glared at the mayor. "We change our decision to not guilty on all charges."

Penn smiled and thanked God for the courage of the jurors. He knew now that those twelve remarkable people would stand by their decision to the end. Penn and his friend would go free.

This proved to be one of the most important legal cases in English history. The mayor jailed and fined the jurors for their verdict. But they appealed to higher courts who ruled that a jury cannot be punished for its verdict. That decision guaranteed the right of English citizens to a fair trial—before a jury who can vote their consciences without being bullied by authorities.

Ten years later, the king gave Penn a large tract of land in America as payment for debts he owed Penn's father. Inspired by his landmark court case, Penn explored the idea of "a holy experiment" on this land. His new colony of Pennsylvania gave common citizens a great deal of say in government and protected the rights of people to worship God as they wished.

Talk about It

- Penn's temper nearly got him in trouble and led him to do things he did not want to do on many occasions. Judging by what happened in this story, what would you tell Penn about controlling his temper? How might that same advice apply to you when you have trouble with your temper?

- Arrange to visit a church of a different denomination with your family. Talk about how others worship God differently from the way your church does. What parts of your worship experience would you not trade for anything, and what are some parts where the differences are not that important? Do you think it's important for everybody to believe and worship the same way?

Prayer

As a family, offer a prayer of thanks for the freedom to worship God and for the things about your own worship service that mean the most to each of you. And don't forget to say thanks for those who sacrificed so we may enjoy that freedom today.

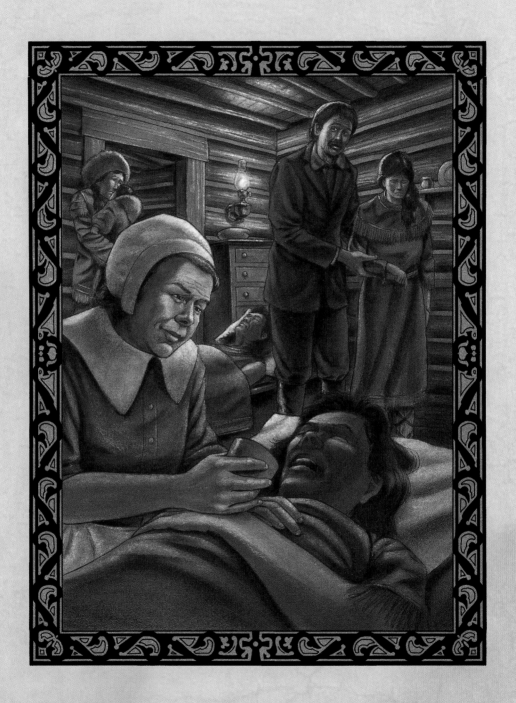

Open House, Open Hearts

GIERTRUD RASCH
1673–1735

 *magine you are forty-five years old. You just gave birth to a child and have three other little ones running around the house. Then your husband, a pastor, announces that he wants the family to leave home and move to a remote outpost on the frozen coast of a foreign land.*

This was the situation Giertrud Rasch (GEAR-trood RASK) faced when her husband wanted to move from their home in Norway to the coast of Greenland. In some ways Rasch was a contemporary woman living in the early eighteenth century. She did not marry until the age of thirty-three (to a man thirteen years younger), and she kept her maiden name all her life. She reacted as most of us might today: She thought her husband, Hans Egede (HAHNS EG-uh-dee), was out of his mind.

So did Egede's bishop. So did the king of Norway—and his voice counted. The king was the head of the church in Norway. When he told Egede to stay home and take care of his family, Egede had to obey. But Egede refused to give up. He quit his job as a parish pastor and spent all his time persuading people to support his missionary effort.

"I DON'T KNOW what that husband of yours is thinking," exclaimed Giertrud's mother, as she rocked her baby granddaughter in her arms. "You and the children living in a sty! Hardly a thing to eat! Why, the children are so skinny they are just wasting away! And if I did not make clothes for you from time to time, I do not know what you would wear!"

Giertrud listened to her mother's long stream of angry complaints. She did not want to speak against her husband. But she had been having her own doubts for a long time. Why had she ever married Hans in the first place? Couldn't she have seen that he was unreliable? The man was determined to ruin his life and the lives of anyone who loved him!

When her mother had gone home, those complaints continued to ring in Giertrud's ears. One night she could bottle it up no longer. She and Hans got into a big argument over his determination to go to Greenland.

"Don't you see?" cried Hans. "How can I claim to be a Christian and not bring souls to Christ? Those people in Greenland need me. I have heard that they were Christian ages ago but have fallen away because they have no pastors."

"But why do you have to be the one to go?" Giertrud argued. "You have a young family to care for. How can you bring your children to such a frozen wilderness? Why not send someone who does not have such responsibilities?"

"I don't know. I am just convinced this is what God has called me to do," said Hans.

"Then perhaps you should do it alone," said Giertrud.

Seeing the determination in her face, his shoulders sagged. Hans looked as though he were at last ready to admit defeat.

"Maybe I am wrong," Hans admitted. "Could we just bring it to the Lord in prayer one last time? Together? Then if you are still opposed, I will give up on going to Greenland."

Giertrud agreed. Maybe this would be the end of that foolish notion. Then, at last, they could get on with their lives.

The two prayed for God to guide them in their future, to show them what God wanted them to do with their lives.

A funny thing happened after that. To her surprise, Giertrud began to sense that God really was calling them to Greenland. When she told this to Hans, he nearly burst with joy. Fueled with a new determination, he finally persuaded the king to send him to Greenland on behalf of the church.

But as the date of their departure grew near, it was Hans who began to have second thoughts.

"What have I gotten you into?" he groaned. "You were right—all of you. The Greenland coast is no place to bring a family. What was I thinking of?"

Giertrud's reply stunned him. "The arrangements are all set," she said. "Did we not already answer God's call and agree to do this? Have faith then that God will bless this venture."

Bolstered by Giertrud's courage, the family set sail for Greenland on March 15, 1720.

Almost as soon as they arrived, Hans realized he had painted too glowing a picture of his mission. The village of Godthaab (GOT-hob) was small and isolated, and it provided few comforts. He had hoped to preach to the descendants of Vikings—distant relatives with whom he would have much in common. Instead, he found only native peoples whose habits and language were foreign to him.

Worst of all, he had imagined that the people would listen to him and joyfully give themselves to Christ. But for the most part, the people did little more than put up with him. Although some of them brought children to be baptized, few seemed interested in his teachings.

As the years went by, Hans often wondered aloud if they had done the right thing in coming. Each time, Giertrud firmly assured him that they had answered God's call.

Hans worked for ten years in Greenland. His efforts to build a church were painfully slow. In April 1730, the Norwegian government decided that his efforts were not worth the expense. It ordered him to come home with his family.

"But we are only now starting to see progress!" Hans protested. "After all the work we put in, how can we leave?"

After Hans stated his case, the government decided to let him stay if he wished. But he must understand that the government would no longer support him. His family would have to survive as best they could.

"So be it," said Giertrud. "We have work to do."

For the next two years, the missionary and his family struggled to survive on a few small donations from friends.

Then, in 1733, disaster struck. One of the Greenlanders made a trip to Denmark. There he caught the deadly disease called smallpox. When he returned to Greenland, he passed the disease on to his friends and family. They, in turn, spread it to their friends and family.

Prior to this time, Greenland had never experienced a terrible epidemic. The people had very little natural immunity to fight off the disease. They had no idea what was causing the disease nor how to contain the outbreak. Fear caused them to imagine terrible things. Some of them began to suspect that there were witches among them who had conjured up the horrible illness. One suspected witch was killed.

Those from infected villages fled in panic to other villages, not realizing that they were carrying the germs with them. By 1734, the smallpox rage struck the village of Godthaab.

Hans watched as many of those he had baptized fell sick with ugly open sores and fevers. It seemed to him that all the people he had brought to Christ with the hope of new life were dying of smallpox. In addition to grief over losing friends, he saw his twelve years of hard work and sacrifice being wiped out before his eyes. Although he did not catch smallpox himself, Hans was so spent from frustration and worry that he could hardly minister at all.

The old doubts came back full force. "We should have left when we had the chance three years ago," he said to Giertrud. "Maybe that was God calling us home."

As always, Giertrud would have none of that. "Perhaps this is what God called us here to do," she said, "to serve a people who are absolutely devastated by disease. I hear some people are throwing the sick out of their houses."

"Not exactly throwing," said Hans. "But, yes, they are putting the sick in the streets. I beg them to show more compassion. But many cannot bear to be around those with such a horrid disease. Others are afraid they will get sick and die if they let those already infected stay with them."

"Then this is a perfect chance for us to reflect the love of Christ," Giertrud said softly. "I would like to open our house to all those who are ill."

Hans's eyes grew huge. "Do you know how many people you are talking about? Our house would be filled with the sick and dying! What about you and the children?"

Giertrud knew the chance she was taking, and it scared her. But if God was not worth taking a chance for, then what good was God anyway? "We are fine for the moment," said Giertrud. "Perhaps we can fill our house with so much love and compassion that we will crowd out the sickness."

Upon Giertrud's insistence, the family opened their house to the sick. Giertrud provided beds for her patients, who soon filled the small living room and then the bedrooms. She rushed from person to person, caring for their never-ending needs. Whether she was easing the suffering of her patients, holding their hands and praying with the dying, or comforting the survivors, Giertrud knew the right thing to say and do.

Finally, the raging disease ran its course. The devastated villages of western Greenland slowly recovered from shock and grief and began to rebuild. At first, Hans Egede did not know what to say to such people. What word of hope could he give after they had experienced such disaster?

But he found that now the people were more eager to listen to him and more willing to take his words to heart. When he commented on the change, one of the Greenlanders told him, "You came to us uninvited and told us what we should do and believe. Many of us did not appreciate that and did not listen to your word. But the kindness shown by your wife moved us. We will never forget how much she has done for us. We would like to know more about the power that drives a person to do such wonderful things."

*G*iertrud Rasch completely wore herself out in the service of God and the Greenlanders. She was already sixty years old at the time of the epidemic and not in good health. Near the end of the smallpox rage, she fell ill herself. After three months of battling the illness, she died. But her compassion and dedication served as an inspiration to her husband, who carried on their work in Greenland.

Talk about It

- Neither Giertrud nor Hans were always entirely sure what God wanted them to do with their lives. Was that a sign that their faith was weak? How do people discover what God wants them to do? How can you know what God's plans are for you?

- Why do you think Giertrud became even more convinced than her husband that they belonged in Greenland. What made Hans doubt his call to Greenland? What finally convinced him in the end?

Prayer

Lord God, show me what you would like me to do with my life. When the path you have set me on proves difficult, strengthen me. When the path seems easy, give me the sense to enjoy and appreciate your world. Amen.

Perils of the South Pacific

JAMES COOK
1728–1779

*H*arbor docks were scenes of tearful farewells when sailors cast off on long ocean voyages in the eighteenth century. Even in the British navy, the world's most advanced fleet at the time, about half of all crew members never returned from their adventures. The greatest danger involved neither fighting nor shipwreck, but a disease known as scurvy. Unlike many sea captains James Cook was determined to do everything in his power to keep his crew healthy.

Perhaps Cook had more sympathy for the common people who made up his crew, because he had grown up in a working-class family. Through long hours of study, he had made himself an expert navigator. This earned him steady promotions in the navy. In 1769, when the British government asked him to lead a long expedition into the uncharted South Pacific, Cook did some research. He paid special attention to the writings of James Lind. Lind had found evidence that scurvy was caused by a poor diet. Captain Cook then crammed his ship, the Endeavour, full of fresh fruit, lemon juice, onions, chickens, sheep, and sauerkraut.

"ARE YOU SURE THIS IS NECESSARY?" grumbled a crewman. He coughed as a cloud of smoke followed him up from the lower deck.

"You are not to question orders," said the officer severely. "When the captain says to build a fire to smoke out the lower deck, you do it. When he says to scrub the decks with vinegar and gunpowder, you do it. It's for your own good, you know. He wants to flush out the bad air and such that can kill sailors. Now get busy!"

Later that day, the officer approached Cook. The captain was directing his men to arrange rows of stools and chairs for the Sunday worship service. Cook saw it his duty as captain to lead regular worship services.

"Place that cloth over the compass box," Cook ordered. "I shall use that as a stand for my Bible and prayer book."

"Captain, pardon me for interrupting," said the officer. "But I heard some of the men saying they will not eat sauerkraut. They say it isn't fit for pigs. Shall I give one or two of them the lash? Make an example of them?"

Cook marked in his Bible the lesson he planned to read and scratched down the name of a hymn to sing. Then he turned to the officer, deep in thought. Sauerkraut was part of the diet that could prevent scurvy. If the crew had seen what Cook had seen— dozens of strong men wasting away from that miserable disease, they would eat the sauerkraut without complaint. But what could he do? He hated to punish the crew.

Suddenly he smiled. "Put out the word that sauerkraut is for officers only. No one else may have any."

The puzzled officer did as Cook asked. Within a week he heard a different kind of grumbling. Some of the crew wanted to know why the officers were being served special food.

"Very well," Cook announced. "The crew have worked hard. They deserve the same food as the officers. From now on, everyone is entitled to sauerkraut."

The officers bit their cheeks to keep from smiling. But Cook's clever plan worked. Convinced that they had earned a rare treat, the sailors began to eat the sauerkraut.

The *Endeavour* sailed for many months. The explorers discovered beautiful and exotic islands and, at Cook's insistence, usually managed to make friends with the inhabitants. They surveyed the coasts of New Zealand and eastern Australia and drew accurate maps of all they saw.

After two years at sea, Cook pointed the *Endeavour* north from the Australian coast and headed for home. He kept a careful watch on what looked like a chalky cluster of rocks just beneath the surface. It was a coral reef—by far the largest Cook had ever seen. The coral, made up of sharp, stony deposits from small sea creatures, was dangerous. The coral's jagged edges could rip a huge hole in the strongest ship bottom. Often it lay only a few feet below the water's surface, where it was difficult to see. For hundreds of miles, the *Endeavour* had been steering a dangerous course through this unending coral reef.

On June 11, Cook went to bed for the night, still wondering when his ship would be free of the coral. He had not slept long when a jolt nearly knocked him out of bed.

The ship had stopped. From the horrid creaking and grating noises, Cook knew instantly what had happened. They had struck the reef and were now stuck on it. Cook tried not to imagine what the sharp coral was doing to his ship's wood.

The captain ran out to the deck. Half the crew had already gathered. Looking out over the moonlit water, he calmly gave orders. "Send out three boats to take soundings," he said calmly. "We need to find out how shallow the coral sits."

When the boats returned from taking soundings, their news was not good. In some spots the coral lay barely three feet below the surface.

"Worse yet," said an officer. "We struck the reef at high tide."

He meant that the level of the water was already at its highest point of the day. As the tide went out, the water level would drop. The *Endeavour* would be even more firmly stuck than it was now.

Cook tried throwing heavy anchors to one side of the reef. He hoped the weight of the anchors would pull the ship loose. But the ship was stuck fast. Afraid that the rescue attempt would tear a hole in the ship, Cook called off the effort.

By early morning, the crew heard more creaks and groans as the ship settled heavily onto the coral. Part of the hull shattered with a crack under the weight of the ship, sending large splinters of wood floating to the surface. The *Endeavour* was starting to break up.

Water began to leak through the holes the coral had punched into the ship bottom. Cook assigned shifts of officers and crew to work pumps that removed the water. Each person worked an exhausting fifteen-minute shift before being replaced.

Cook knew that he was facing almost certain disaster. Not that he was worried about drowning. The shore was only a few miles away, and they could probably float there on the broken pieces of wood. But all their food and supplies would go down with the ship. They could be stranded on some forsaken bit of land 12,000 miles from home. No one in England would know where to find them. Even if they survived, they would probably never see home again.

But Cook let none of his fear show. "Lighten her up, boys!" he cried. "Everything that is not absolutely necessary goes overboard."

Inspired by their captain's courage, the crew laughed and chattered as they hauled cannon balls and dropped them into the water. Several of them began wheeling the thousand-pound cannons to the side of the boat. Six of these huge iron weapons fell into the water with a tremendous splash. By the time they were finished, the crew had pitched 100,000 pounds of equipment into the sea.

Meanwhile, the crew worked furiously all day long to pump out water that was pouring through the leaks. Cook waited anxiously as the tide rose. Would the ship now float over the coral?

No! It was still too heavy.

Late in the afternoon, the ship slid and settled on another section of coral. The *Endeavour* began tilting to the side. Soon it would capsize and then everything would be lost.

"Captain, the situation is hopeless!" cried an officer. "The water is coming in so fast the pumps cannot keep up with it."

Cook saw that he had no choice but to risk everything on one last gamble. "Throw the anchors out again," he said. "This time, pull until we are off."

The officer nodded grimly. He knew the risk they were taking. By pulling the ship hard across the sharp coral, they could rip the bottom right off. The ship would fill up so fast that most of the crew would drown.

The crew dropped the anchors. Cook listened intently as the lightened ship began to slide across the coral. Suddenly, with a great wrenching sound, the ship broke loose. They were now free but still in serious trouble. Although the coral had not sliced open the ship, it had ripped a gaping hole.

Sweating and grunting, the crew worked furiously at the pumps. But the water level continued to rise. The ship was going down fast.

Cook had one last trick up his sleeve, a trick he learned from one of his crew. "We need to patch that hole," he said firmly. "Take a twenty-foot section of sail and smear it with sheep dung. Then take another section of sail and plaster it against the other."

It was not the most pleasant job, but the crew did not hesitate to carry out the order. Following Cook's instructions, they lowered the sail sections into the ocean. Swimmers then pulled the sails across the hole in the ship bottom. The force of the water rushing into the boat pinned the sail in place and the dung stopped most of the water from leaking in.

A cheer rose from the crew. They were able to sail the *Endeavour* to shore. There they pulled a large section of coral from the hole and repaired the damage.

An officer looked at the captain in admiration. "After such a close call, I believe we shall have perfect attendance at your next prayer service," he said.

*I*t had taken cool leadership and many strong backs to keep the Endeavour *from sinking. Most ships that had been at sea for two years would not have had enough strong, healthy bodies to work the pumps around the clock. Thanks to Cook's care for his crew's well-being, the* Endeavour's *crew was up to the task.*

When the ship finally sailed into port in England, 117 of its original 118 crew members walked off to greet their families. Not one crew member died of disease during the three-year voyage.

Talk about It

- People in leadership positions must demonstrate to others that they are in command. Many leaders do this by showing how tough they are. How did Cook demonstrate his leadership? What qualities do you think make for a good leader?

- Some people think that kindness is a sign of weakness. Is that ever true? How much do you value the trait of kindness in your friends?

Prayer

Jesus, our Savior, whose name we praise,
Teach us your kind and gentle ways.
Help us to show our love for you
By letting it shine through in all we do. Amen

The *Singer Who Saw Stars*

CAROLINE HERSCHEL
1750-1848

*W*ho would have thought playing an oboe could get a person into such trouble? Yet it forced William Herschel (HER-shul) to leave his country! Herschel had the misfortune to be playing in the Hanover (now part of Germany) army band when the French captured the town in 1757. Afraid of being taken prisoner, William fled to England. There he found work as a church organist in a well-to-do resort area.

The French eventually left Hanover and, many years later, William returned to visit his family. He felt sorry for his younger sister, Caroline, who was stuck cooking and cleaning for her parents and for another grown-up brother. Although she never complained, the constant housework prevented her from following her dream of being a professional singer.

William wanted to help her. In 1772, he brought his twenty-two-year-old sister to England to serve as his housekeeper. In her spare time, Caroline could train her voice with help from her musical brother. For a brief time, Caroline's singing career began to blossom. But then William became more and more fascinated with his hobby: astronomy.

CAROLINE PEEKED IN THE DOOR and found William huddled over a cluttered desk. He was polishing a new lens for one of his homemade telescopes.

"I should have known you would be here," she said. "Do you know your supper is cold again?"

William did not even look up from his work. "I'm sorry, but I am right in the middle of something," he said.

"You are always in the middle of something," noted Caroline. "I suppose you can skip your supper. But what about the Octagon Chapel choir? Did you forget about rehearsal?"

This time William glanced up. His mouth flew open. "You're right! How could I forget?" He paused and looked at his work. "Oh, dear! But if I quit now . . ."

Caroline sighed. She had planned to work on her voice lessons this evening, but she could not bear to see her brother upset. "Never mind. I shall direct the choir for you tonight so you can finish. Again."

"Oh, thank you," William said. "I shall make this up to you."

No, you won't, thought Caroline. William was becoming so involved with his astronomy hobby that he barely had time for his profession. He never composed music anymore. He had fewer music students each year. Caroline was doing practically all the music copying and choir directing that had been part of William's job.

Sometimes Caroline grumbled to herself about his selfish hobby. "What about my singing career?" she wanted to ask. "Why do I always seem to be so busy with your things that I have no time for mine?"

But every time she made up her mind to approach William on the subject, he would rush in to describe his latest discovery. He was so thrilled by what he had found that she did not have the heart to burst his bubble. Besides, looking at his work, she got the feeling that William was making some important scientific discoveries. She had heard friends say that no one in all of England had telescopes as good as William's.

As the months passed, William became so obsessed with astronomy that Caroline grew concerned. When he missed every meal one day, Caroline carried his supper up to his observing post. She found William on a ladder at his largest telescope amid a jumble of ropes, pulleys, and scaffolding. "William, you have been at this for sixteen hours straight," she said. "You must take some time to eat."

"I cannot spare the time just now," William insisted.

"If it were not for cloudy nights and full moons that make stargazing impossible, I do not think you would ever sleep," Caroline said. Undaunted, she climbed up next to him on the ladder. "Open your mouth," she said.

Without taking his eyes off his work, William opened his mouth and let Caroline feed him.

When she finished, she climbed down and opened a book called *The Arabian Nights*. "If you must stay at your post," she said, settling into a chair, "perhaps I can read some stories to help you stay awake."

After a time, Caroline began looking for other ways to help. Under William's training, she learned how to grind glass for his telescope lenses. She watched the precise way in which he recorded his observations. Before long, she was sitting up with William long past midnight, making notes of his observations.

On one occasion William's do-it-yourself hobby nearly got them both killed. William wanted to build larger and larger telescopes so that he could see farther out into space. He needed very large, precisely measured pieces of glass and metal for these telescopes. When no one could provide him with these materials, he decided to forge them in his basement.

He and Caroline, along with a couple of helpers, hand-formed the large molds into which molten glass or metal would be poured. Once, when they were pouring metal into a mold, the mold cracked. Glowing molten metal spilled out onto the stone floor. The intense heat caused the stones to shatter. The Herschels raced upstairs to safety while stone shards and liquid metal flew all around them.

At times like this, Caroline thought wistfully about her dream of being a singer. But William was so thrilled to have her as his assistant that he totally forgot about her career plans.

On a dark night in March of 1781, William was studying a section of the sky when he noticed something unusual. What at first looked like a star did not act like a star. Stars kept their brightness no matter how much he magnified them with his telescope. This object grew dull and blurry under his high-powered lenses. William decided it must be a comet.

He called out to Caroline, who recorded the precise location of the object, the time, and William's descriptions. William then wrote up these notes in an article he had published entitled "Account of a Comet."

Few astronomers had ever heard of William Herschel, but several of them were interested enough in his findings to check out this new heavenly object. Within a few months came astounding news. What Herschel thought was a comet turned out to be a planet in our very own solar system! Astronomers had thought all the planets had been discovered long ago.

This find brought William instant fame. Many astronomers wanted to name the new planet after its discoverer. But William modestly declined, and it was named "Uranus."

King George of England rewarded William by making him the official royal astronomer. For the first time, William could work full time at his favorite task. Not only did the king provide him with money for a top observatory, but he also agreed to pay Caroline to work as William's assistant. It was a bittersweet moment for Caroline. She knew this new position meant that, once and for all, her career as a singer was over. But she was thrilled that her brother had such an important position.

"I have you to thank for much of my success," William told her. "You know, you are very good at observing stars. You should take some time to explore the heavens on your own."

"And if I did that, who would help you?" she asked.

"I must go to Germany next week to meet with other learned astronomers," he answered. "While I am gone, why don't you see what you can find in those telescopes?"

Caroline accepted the challenge. On a clear night, she climbed up to the flat-topped roof of her apartment. She looked at the polished telescope in front of her. *It was a beautiful, precise instrument,* she thought, *very much like a musical instrument.* As she scanned the skies with the telescope, she marveled at how the heavens were like a musical composition. The stars were like notes—each had its place in creating a splendid work of art. God had created both music and the night sky and had made them marvelous beyond words. Maybe, just maybe, she was not so far off from her musical career after all.

After a few hours of gazing, her trained eye spotted another of those "stars" that did not quite act like a star. She made notes on the position of the object in the sky and reported it to William when he returned.

After reviewing her information, William smiled broadly at her. "Congratulations! You have discovered a new comet!"

Caroline became such an expert at astronomy that William relied heavily on her. When he discovered some errors in a famous catalog of stars, he asked Caroline to double-check all the information in the catalog. The painstaking task took her twenty months. But her findings, which were published in 1798, corrected hundreds of errors in the old catalog.

Long after William died, Caroline was invited to a reception to meet the crown prince of Prussia. She was ninety-seven years of age and quite frail. But she walked to the center of the hall with a proud determination in her step.

Caroline bowed ever so slightly. "If you please, Your Highness," she said. "You know my brother and me as astronomers. But there was a time when we both had different dreams. I would like to sing for you a song written by my brother more than fifty years ago."

In a voice shaky with age yet clear, she began to sing. As Caroline Herschel looked out over her audience, she thought for a moment of what might have been. She could have been standing here when she was young and beautiful and her voice strong and lovely. But the thought did not make her sad at all. She felt nothing but love for her brother and no regrets for the sacrifice she had made.

In her own limited time as an explorer of the skies, Caroline Herschel discovered eight comets. Most of her devoted efforts were spent making it possible for William Herschel to become one of the greatest astronomers of all time.

Talk about It

- Why did Caroline allow her dream to get sidetracked? Who was to blame for this? Would you call the story of Caroline Herschel a sad story or a happy one?

- Have you ever had your heart set on something that just never worked out—perhaps because you got sidetracked by responsibilities or obligations? How did you feel? How did Caroline deal with disappointment?

Prayer

God, we ask your special blessing on those who work unnoticed in the background to make life easier or more successful for those they love. Help us appreciate their efforts. Grant them peace and the understanding that they are as important as anyone in doing God's work on earth. Amen.

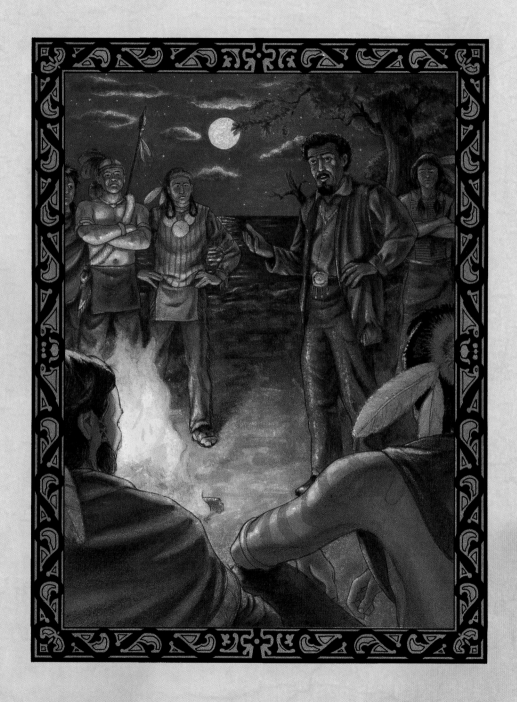

The Honest Trader
& a Deathbed Wish

JEAN BAPTISTE DUSABLE
1750–1818

veryone who saw the plain of Eschikagou (es-chih-KAH-goh) thought it was an ideal place for a settlement. It stood where the Great Lakes connected to the Mississippi River and would attract a great deal of trade.

But the land was an ancient battleground for warring tribes of Native Americans. If Illinois or Miami Indians passing through the area ran into their enemies, the Ottawa or Potawatomi (pah-tuh-WAH-tuh-mee), fighting broke out. Nor did the tribes welcome outsiders into the battle zone. The British claimed that same land as part of their American empire. But they did not want to fight all the powerful tribes in the area if they could find an easier way of gaining control of the land.

This was the situation when Jean Baptiste DuSable (ZHAHN bap-TEEST Duh-SAH-bluh) left Haiti in 1764. Along with his best friend, Jacques Clemorgan, DuSable loaded a small ship with coffee and lumber from their plantations. The young men planned to sell the goods in New Orleans. They could then use the money to start a business in the New World.

THE WIND ROARED OUT OF THE EAST, nearly blowing Jean DuSable off the deck. Ocean waves swelled up and smashed into the side of the boat. DuSable looked anxiously toward the distant coastline. They had come so close to reaching America. But he doubted his heavily loaded ship could survive this hurricane.

Just as he feared, a huge wave slammed into the ship. It swept the entire crew, including DuSable, into the ocean. DuSable fought his way to the surface. Through salt-stung eyes, he saw his splintered ship tossing upside down in the waves. Then he caught sight of Clemorgan struggling to stay afloat.

Gasping for breath as the waves pounded him, DuSable pulled his friend toward land. After two exhausting hours of swimming, they reached the sandy shore. He had no idea where he was or how to get help.

The storm quickly blew over. The next morning DuSable looked out to sea and saw a ship in the distance. "I'll be right back," he told Clemorgan.

DuSable swam until he was out of sight. Clemorgan was afraid his friend had drowned. But finally a small boat paddled in to shore. DuSable had reached the ship and found help.

The ship took the two men to New Orleans. But with their cargo lost at sea, they owned nothing but the clothes they wore. Clemorgan, who was white, found a job as a clerk. But DuSable was black, and New Orleans was not a safe place for a black man. Even though he was a French citizen, someone might try to claim him as a runaway slave. Fearful of causing trouble for Clemorgan, DuSable stayed hidden. But without money or food, he grew desperate. Finally, he staggered into a mission run by Father Gibault (zhee-BOH).

The kindly priest fed and housed DuSable for nearly a year. In exchange, DuSable tended the mission's garden. One day while weeding the garden, DuSable spotted an Indian named Choctaw, who was half-dead from starvation. Fur traders from the north had hired him to guide them to New Orleans. But once Choctaw had brought them to the city, the traders sent him away with nothing.

DuSable brought Choctaw into the mission, and the two became friends. Choctaw told him about the rich lands to the north. The forests there were full of fur-bearing animals. As he listened, DuSable grew excited. Why not go into the fur-trading business together? Clemorgan could join them, too.

Father Gibault supported their plan. He gave them food and other supplies. As they parted, DuSable thanked the priest. "I don't know what I would have done without you," he said. "I promise I will pay you back one day."

Father Gibault shrugged. "You owe me nothing. Just repay God with good works. I think God has great plans for you."

The three men—one black, one white, one Indian—paddled up the Mississippi River to the frontier town of St. Louis. There they set up their base for trapping operations. With Choctaw's expert advice, the men were able to gather many fine furs. Their business did so well that soon DuSable opened a trading post.

Indians needed many of the goods that DuSable had to sell. But they had no money. All they could offer were the furs they had trapped. That was fine with DuSable. He bought their furs and had Clemorgan resell them on his trips to New Orleans. Unlike earlier traders in the area, DuSable dealt fairly with the Indians. His reputation for honesty spread. Indians came from miles away to deal with the trader they could trust.

One of DuSable's admirers was an old Ottawa chief named Pontiac. Pontiac had once been the most feared warrior of the Midwest. English settlers shuddered at the mention of his name. But he made peace in his later years and promised he would fight no more.

In May of 1769, an Ottawa messenger approached DuSable with shocking news. An Illinois brave had sneaked into Pontiac's lodge during the night and stabbed the old chief. Pontiac now lay near death. He had asked to see DuSable and Choctaw.

The men hurried to Pontiac's village. They found the great chief lying on a bearskin blanket. "The Ottawa and our allies, the Potawatomi, will seek revenge against the Illinois for my murder," Pontiac said.

"That is so," said Choctaw. "Such treachery surely must be punished."

"No," said Pontiac weakly. "I believe the man who stabbed me was sent by the British to stir war among us. Open warfare between our tribes will destroy us. We will become so weak that the British can walk in and take our lands without a fight."

DuSable nodded. "What do you want me to do?"

"I cannot bear to think that my death will harm my people," said Pontiac. "You alone are respected by all Indians in these lands. Talk to the war councils of the Potawatomi and the Ottawa. Choctaw will guide you to them. Persuade them to make peace with the Illinois."

DuSable doubted he could talk the Indians out of war. But he could not refuse his dying friend's request.

For weeks, DuSable and Choctaw canoed up the Mississippi and Illinois Rivers. It was a tense time. The murder of Pontiac had put all Indians on edge. The canoers passed many villages of Illinois Indians who watched them suspiciously.

At last they reached the portage of Eschikagou. (A portage is land where canoes are carried between rivers or lakes.) DuSable thought it was the most beautiful place he had ever seen.

"What a shame this is a battleground between Indians," he thought. "I would love to settle here."

They entered Lake Michigan and paddled up the shore until they reached a great Potawatomi camp. DuSable tried to find the words to persuade the angry Indians to put away their weapons. But as he expected, the Potawatomi chief refused his request. "Every Potawatomi and Ottawa demands revenge. How can I go against their wishes?" he said.

DuSable argued and pleaded. Finally, the chief said, "I will not seek peace. But I will ask the chiefs at the war council to let you speak. If you persuade them, I will go along."

The Ottawa and their allies traveled from hundreds of miles to attend this council. When DuSable saw the determination and anger in their eyes, he wondered why he should waste his time speaking.

The Potawatomi chief introduced DuSable. "This man wears the honor belt of Pontiac," he said. "That great man asked him on his deathbed to speak to our council. Please hear him."

"He may speak," said the chiefs. "But he must be quick. We have much to do to plan our revenge against the Illinois."

DuSable stood and told them of his peace mission. The Indians cried out in rage. "The knife that killed Pontiac must have poisoned his mind!" one shouted.

DuSable was ready to give up. "They will never listen," he thought. "I should quit before they turn on me."

But he remembered the sadness in Pontiac's eyes. He remembered the words of Father Gibault: "God has plans for you. Repay him with good works."

DuSable spoke more urgently to the Indians, warning them that war against the Illinois would play into the hands of the British. "Your stubbornness will cost you your lands."

A few Indians seemed to be considering these words. "There is no dishonor in peace," DuSable continued. "To forgive an enemy takes courage. The great Pontiac, who feared nothing and whom all others feared, asked this of you. He did so out of love for his people."

When DuSable finished speaking, the Indians sat in silence. Finally, one said, "The man who wears the honor belt of Pontiac speaks as a friend of Indians. He has convinced me to do what he asked." The others agreed, many reluctantly.

DuSable left the campfire weak with relief.

Choctaw caught up to him, smiling in disbelief. "You did it!" he said. "No other person in the world could have brought peace here tonight."

"Just repaying a debt," DuSable said smiling.

"Now that your mission is done, shall we return to St. Louis?" Choctaw asked.

DuSable thought for a moment. "No. Now that the Indians are at peace, perhaps they will let me build a cabin. At Eschikagou."

In 1772, Jean DuSable built a cabin along the Eschikagou portage. The Indians never disturbed him. The deadly battleground became a thriving settlement. Even when troubles arose between Indians and settlers in 1813, the Indians remembered DuSable. Although they burned most of the settlement, they left the former buildings of DuSable untouched. The name of the settlement that DuSable started was eventually shortened from Eschikagou to Chicago, now one of the largest cities in the world.

Talk about It

- Why did DuSable care so much—even to the point of risking his life—about whether the Indians went to war? What did he have to gain from preventing war?

- In many ways, the story of DuSable is a story about getting even—both for good and for evil. As DuSable learned, we cannot always repay people for the things they do for us, or to us. What lesson did he learn from the priest's advice? What did Pontiac teach him about repaying people? Have you ever tried to get even with someone you felt wronged you? How did it turn out?

Prayer

Almighty God, we know we can never repay you for the love you have shown us. Help us remember that the best way to respond to your love is to share it with others. Amen.

A Question of Honor

SACAGAWEA
1784?–1812

hen President Thomas Jefferson bought the Louisiana Territory for the United States in 1803, he had little idea what he was getting from France for his three million dollars. No white person had ever seen parts of this new land, particularly the area west of what is now North and South Dakota.

Jefferson asked Captain Merriwether Lewis and Captain William Clark to lead an expedition to explore this territory. Their plan was to travel by boat as far west as they could go up the Missouri River. At that point, they would try to buy horses—mostly likely from the Shoshone (shoh-SHOH-nee) Indians—and continue on horseback.

When Lewis and Clark got as far as Fort Mandan (North Dakota), they hired a trapper named Charbonneau (SHAR-buh-noh) and his wife, Sacagawea (SACK-uh-juh-WEE-uh) as interpreters and guides. Sacagawea was a Shoshone Indian who had been kidnapped from her people when she was twelve. Charbonneau had won her as a prize in a gambling game. Lewis and Clark figured the young woman would be useful when it came time to bargain with the Shoshone for horses.

LEWIS AND CLARK WALKED ALONG the grassy shore, scouting the land. To their left, a large boat fought against the current of the Missouri River. Charbonneau, the trapper, was steering the boat. His wife sat near him.

Lewis and Clark still did not know much about these late additions to their party. Sacagawea had turned out to be a godsend. "Janey," as Clark affectionately called her, had taught the men to poke sharp sticks in the burrows of these strange little prairie-dog creatures and dig out wild artichokes. She also knew a lot about seeds and berries. Without her wilderness wisdom, the men would have gone to bed hungry many a night.

Charbonneau was a different story. He hadn't shown much skill as a guide, and the leaders wondered if he would be any good as an interpreter. One thing they did know about him—he was easily the worst boatsman in the entire expedition.

Without warning, a low, heavy bank of clouds blotted out the sun. Powerful winds swirled across the plain. Before the boat could get to shore, the skies opened in a tremendous downpour. A vicious gust lifted up one side of Charbonneau's boat, and it tipped so far that water began pouring over the sides.

Lewis and Clark watched in horror as the boat filled with water. Wooden cases filled with valuable scientific instruments, books, and supplies spilled out into the river.

"Help! Help!" screamed Charbonneau. "I can't swim! We're going to drown!" In panic he let go of the tiller used to steer, and clung to the side. The boat floundered in the open water.

"I'll drown you myself if you don't take the tiller!" shouted one of the men in front. The rest of the men began bailing water for all they were worth.

Meanwhile, Sacagawea calmly reached into the choppy current. One by one, she caught the cases and pulled them back into the boat. By the time Charbonneau finally steered the boat to the bank, she had retrieved almost all of them.

Once again, thought Clark, Sacagawea is the one out of that couple who is earning the money. Had she not saved those instruments, the expedition would have had difficulty trying to map their travels. Even Lewis, who hadn't paid much attention to the young woman, began to treat her with new respect.

Eventually, the explorers came to the headwaters of the Missouri River. They had reached the critical stage of their journey. If they could not get horses here, they would probably have to turn back. If they could not make friends with the Indians, they could be wiped out.

Unsure of which route to take, they split up. Lewis and a few others headed away from the river into the hills. Clark, Charbonneau, and Sacagawea traveled along the edge of a shallow river. As the latter group approached a valley, Sacagawea felt a tingling in her veins. She knew this spot! This was the place where she had been captured by the Hidatsa Indians years ago. This was the last place she had been among her own people.

In the evening a messenger arrived with news from Lewis.

"Captain Lewis found a band of Shoshone," said the messenger. "I think he scared them at first because they ran off. But he kept after them and somehow got them to understand that we're friendly."

"Where is he now?" asked Clark.

"The Shoshone invited him to their camp. He wants you to hurry over there first thing in the morning. He's having a terrible time making himself understood."

Early the next morning, Sacagawea set off with the others to join Lewis. She could hardly wait to get to the Shoshone camp. Perhaps she would hear some word of her family.

As they reached the outskirts of the village, she studied the faces of those they met. Suddenly she stopped and gasped. That face! Could it be . . . ?

Sacagawea hopped and danced with excitement. With a cry of joy she ran to a young woman and wrapped her arms around her. It was her best friend from years ago—the girl with whom she had been walking when the Hidatsa carried her away. Sacagawea thought the girl had been killed.

After the brief reunion, the group continued into the village. They were escorted to a tent. Here they found Lewis trying to explain with hand gestures to a Shoshone chief that he wanted horses and was willing to pay for them.

Lewis sighed with relief when he saw his interpreters. Calling Sacagawea to sit by his side, he said, "I get the feeling he knows what I want but isn't too eager to give up his horses. I want you to explain to him . . ."

But Sacagawea heard nothing he said. How could she pay attention to Lewis when she recognized the chief as her own brother, Cameahwait (kuh-MEE-uh-wait)? For the second time that day, Sacagawea squealed with excitement. She threw her blanket over her brother and hugged him.

It proved a bittersweet reunion. Sacagawea's brother told her that the years had treated her family harshly. All members of her family were dead except Cameahwait and one other brother.

Furthermore, although the presence of his sister had eased the chief's fears of the white men, he was still reluctant to part with his horses. As Sacagawea explained to Lewis, the expedition had not brought much of value to trade for them. The Indians were not interested in money nor in the other trinkets the white men offered.

Sacagawea knew how much her traveling companions were depending on the horses. She quietly slipped off her blue-beaded belt. The beautiful belt was about the only thing of value that

Sacagawea owned. Yet she offered it to Lewis to use in trade. Eventually, Lewis and Clark produced enough of value to purchase the horses they needed to continue their exploration.

That night, Sacagawea could not sleep. For the first time since she was a girl, she was home among her people. She wanted to stay awake and drink in all the sights and sounds. As she wandered through the village in the shadows of night, she heard her brother talking with other braves.

The Indians did not feel comfortable with these strange visitors. The Shoshone needed to hunt food for their families and could not afford to waste time talking with strangers. But neither did they want to fight with them, especially since the strangers were friends with Sacagawea.

Cameahwait finally decided they should simply slip away from the white men. Tomorrow afternoon they would leave camp, taking all their horses with them.

Sacagawea walked back to her tent deeply disturbed. She had so looked forward to this meeting with her people, and now she almost wished she had not come. Her traveling companions desperately needed the horses, and the Shoshone had agreed to sell them. The captains must be warned what Cameahwait planned to do. Perhaps they could make him change his mind before it was too late.

On the other hand, the Shoshone were her people. How could she take sides against her own flesh and blood? Why should she warn the white men? She was with them only because of her husband, and he had always treated her poorly—more like a slave than a wife.

But then Captain Clark had always treated her well—almost like a friend.

All night long, Sacagawea brooded about what she should do. In the morning, she still had not decided. Whenever she thought she had reached a decision, she saw the other side of the argument and changed her mind.

Finally, the time came when she knew the Shoshone would be stealing away. There could be no more delay. She had to make up her mind.

In the end, Sacagawea decided that doing the right thing was more important than protecting her family. Cameahwait had made an agreement with Lewis and Clark. Those men were counting on him to live up to it. If her people could not be trusted to keep their word, then the tragedy and violence that had befallen her own family would only get worse.

Late that afternoon, Sacagawea went to Charbonneau. "Cameahwait is planning to leave with the horses," she said.

"What?" exclaimed Charbonneau. "When? We'd better tell Captain Lewis quickly."

Informed of Cameahwait's plan, Lewis and Clark caught up with the chief before he and his warriors disappeared. They persuaded him to honor his word.

Thanks to Sacagawea, the Lewis and Clark expedition had the horses to continue west.

The Lewis and Clark expedition reached the Pacific Ocean safely in November of 1805 and returned to President Jefferson with valuable information on this newly purchased land.

Talk about It

- How would you have felt in Sacagawea's position? Have you ever been in a similar situation? For example, have you ever been with friends who wanted to be mean to a person who had been cruel or unfair to you? How did you handle the situation? How did you feel afterward?

- Have each member of your family make a list of Christian values that are most important to you—things such as keeping your promises or being kind to everyone. Compare your lists and then combine them into a family list: "What our family values most." Post your list where everyone can see it.

Prayer

Ask God always to help you remember what is truly important. Pray for guidance in making decisions that truly reflect the will of God.

Fugitive in a Strange Land

ANN JUDSON
1789-1826

nn Hasseltine was in desperate need of a husband for a rather unusual reason. Since opening her heart to Christ at a New England revival meeting, she had wanted to go overseas as a missionary. But American churches did not think much of sending missionaries to dangerous lands. Allowing a single woman to take on the risk was out of the question.

Fortunately, she found a young man with a craving to preach the gospel to the Asian land of Burma. She and Adoniram Judson were married and then sailed for the Far East in February 1812.

Their ship docked at Calcutta, India, at the end of a four-month voyage. The Judsons could hardly have chosen a worse time to set foot in that country. India was governed by Great Britain, with whom the United States had just begun to fight a war. Furthermore, the powerful East India Company dictated many of the decisions of the British government in Asia. This trading company did not care for missionaries; they feared missionaries would attack native religions and stir up resentment. The locals might lash out at all Europeans, including the East India Company.

WITH EACH NEW DAY, the news got worse.

"Burma is out of the question," said Carey, the old missionary who was hosting the Judsons in Calcutta until they got settled. "Those people hate missionaries and they are brutal."

Although disappointed, Adoniram simply said, "Then we shall find others out here who need to hear God's word."

"God has sent us to Asia for a purpose," said Ann confidently.

Her confidence was soon shaken, however. That afternoon a messenger arrived with a notice that the Judsons were wanted by the Calcutta police.

Sweltering in the July heat, the Judsons reported to the police station. A police officer greeted them stiffly. After escorting them into his office, he pulled out a sheet of paper. "By order of the British government, you are instructed to leave India and return home at once," he read. "The ship on which you arrived is due to sail tomorrow. The captain has been told he may not leave unless you are aboard."

Ann was stunned. She had been so certain that God had called them to be missionaries. After all the expense and time and effort of traveling to India, how could they just pack up and go home without having accomplished anything?

After asking a lot of questions, the Judsons found a possible solution. They agreed to leave India. But instead of returning home, they would sail for the Isle of France, off the coast of Africa. With luck, a mission field would open up for them while they bided their time there.

One problem remained: the British government in India did not give them a passport to sail to the Isle of France. The Judsons sat around for four months waiting. Finally, in late November, the British closed the door on this possibility.

"You are to leave at once on an East India Company ship bound for England," the police told them. "No excuses this time."

Desperate for some alternative, the Judsons rushed to the river port. There they discovered a ship, called the *Creole*, that was bound for the Isle of France.

"Could you please take us?" the Judsons asked the pilot.

"Sure," he said, "as long as you have a passport."

Adoniram sighed heavily. "The British won't give us one. Please, please, will you take us anyway?"

The captain shrugged. He could use their money. They seemed like nice folks. "I can't take you on board without a passport. But," he smiled secretively, "if I found you on the ship after we cast off, I don't suppose I would kick you off."

Thrilled, the Judsons rushed to pack their bags. At midnight, they and Luther Rice, a friend who was in the same situation, crept through the streets with all their luggage. When they arrived safely at the dock, they found it almost deserted. Quickly they stowed away aboard the *Creole*.

The pilot seemed pleased to see them when they appeared on deck the next morning.

"At last we're through with the British," Ann thought as they headed down the river.

But two days later, just before they reached the ocean, a boat sped toward them. Ann's heart sank as she saw the British flag on the boat. "You have fugitives on board," called a government official. "You may not sail further until they are off."

"How did they find us?" she wondered.

Adoniram thought quickly. "Luther and I shall get off now. Maybe that will satisfy them. You stay hidden on board. We shall try to sneak back on at night."

But the British were wary of this couple's tricks. The pilot was not allowed to proceed until he would swear that no unauthorized persons were still aboard. Reluctantly he brought Ann to the British.

"I cannot understand it," Adoniram moaned as they sat in a dreary tavern on the edge of the river. "Why does God not allow us to do the work he has called us to do?"

"It is a mystery to me also," said Ann. "But let us not give up hope. God is not thwarting us; men are. God will find a way to beat even the most determined of men."

"I am not giving up," said Adoniram, "although at this point I'm not sure what else we can do. All I can think of is to avoid the authorities as long as possible. Perhaps we should quietly get away. Move downstream a ways."

He had heard that there was a small inn about sixteen miles downriver. They would go there and decide what to do next. As they prepared to leave, however, they remembered their luggage. The boat that had taken them to shore had been too small to carry it. Ann offered to find a slightly larger boat that would take her to the *Creole* and fetch the luggage.

By this time the weather had turned nasty. As Ann's boat chased after the *Creole*, strong gusts of wind nearly capsized it. Rolling waves tossed the boat so badly that Ann was dizzy and sick to her stomach by the time they caught up to the boat.

Seeing her pitiful condition, the pilot refused to let her go back in the smaller boat. "I will take you and your luggage to the inn," he offered. That had not been the plan, but Ann was too sick to refuse. She sent the smaller boat back with instructions that Adoniram was to meet her at the inn.

A few hours later, she sat in the inn—more accurately, a shabby tavern. She still felt queasy from the boat ride.

Never in her life had she felt so alone and so helpless. Suddenly she realized the risk she had taken in changing their plans. Had Adoniram gotten her message? What if he hadn't? How would she find him? If she didn't, how would she manage all alone in this strange land?

She looked at the faces around her. How terrifying to be alone in a place where you cannot speak the language and do not know the customs!

Whenever someone looked at her, she tried to melt back into the shadows. With the British looking for her, she wanted to avoid any kind of attention. But with her white skin and light hair, she stuck out like a candle in the darkness. Any of these people could betray her at any moment.

More horrifying thoughts gnawed at her. What if the British found her and hauled her off before Adoniram arrived? What if the British had already caught her husband? What if something worse had happened to him on his way to the inn?

Ann took a deep breath. "I will not panic," she told herself. "God is my strength. He will not fail me. No matter how bad it looks, I believe God will make things turn out."

For many hours she waited, chasing away doubts and fears that kept creeping back into her mind. Whenever she felt herself giving way to fear, she prayed. At last, in the darkness, she saw Adoniram coming down the road. Ann ran to him and hugged him until he thought he would suffocate.

They hid out for three days at the inn, wondering where to go next. But then the moment they had both dreaded came. A policeman found them sitting at a table in the inn. Without a word, he plopped a letter in front of them.

Adoniram's heart sank. Dejectedly he opened the letter. Ann sat quietly across from him, waiting for the bad news.

But Adoniram's eyebrows shot up. "Ann, look at this!"

The letter was an official government pass giving them permission to travel on the *Creole*.

"Where did it come from? Who sent it?" asked Ann.

"I don't have the slightest idea," said Adoniram. Then more quietly he said, "Actually, I think we both know who sent it: God.

I don't know how or why, but such a miracle can only come from God."

Suddenly his joyful grin disappeared. "But it is too late! The *Creole* left three days ago. Surely, it has gone out to sea by now! Why couldn't this have arrived sooner?"

Ann refused to be discouraged. "Do not lose your faith in God. Something marvelous is at work here. Somehow I have the feeling the *Creole* is not out of range yet. Hurry, let's find a boat and catch it."

The Judsons hired the fastest boat they could find. Hour after hour, they stared into the horizon as the boat sped downriver, hoping to see the *Creole*. Sure enough, just before the river opened into the ocean, they found the *Creole* at anchor, ready to cast off. The ship had been waiting two days for crew members who were unexpectedly late in reaching the ship.

After feeling the presence of God so closely in their escape from India, the Judsons found the courage to tackle the forbidding mission field of Burma. Ann Judson spent fourteen years in Burma translating, teaching, and sharing her faith before dying of a tropical fever. She once described the sighting of the anchored Creole *they were chasing as "the sweetest moment of my life."*

Talk about It

- Many times the Judsons must have felt almost abandoned—even by God. Yet they refused to give up their mission, deciding instead to pray harder and to encourage each other. How do we know when it might be time to give up on a goal and when we should just pray harder and encourage one another to keep trying?

- Does our faith in God mean everything will work out the way we think God wants it to? If not, just what does trust in God mean?

Things to Do

Read Psalm 23 aloud. Then say a special prayer for missionaries in foreign lands. If your church sponsors a missionary or a missionary family, find out as much as you can about them and pray for their health and their needs and their success.

Lady Jane & the Fate of Sir John

JANE FRANKLIN
1792–1875

 he search for a water route across North America to the Pacific Ocean (the "Northwest Passage") was one of the most frustrating exercises in the history of exploration. Nearly two centuries after Marquette and Jolliet ruled out the Mississippi River, the British were still looking.

On May 19, 1845, Sir John Franklin set sail from London on yet another quest for the Northwest passage. He hoped to find it in the icy waters of the unexplored Canadian territories above the Arctic Circle.

At fifty-eight years of age, Franklin was rather old for such a grueling, hazardous voyage. His wife, Lady Jane Franklin, must have fretted about this as she watched his two ships, the Erebus and the Terror, sail off. She comforted herself with the knowledge that Franklin had played a lead role in two other explorations of the frozen Canadian wilderness.

In the autumn of 1845, a ship returned to London with news that Sir John's two ships had been sighted sailing in north Baffin Bay. All seemed well. But as months dragged into years with no further word, Lady Jane grew anxious.

DRESSED IN HER FINEST CLOTHES, Jane Franklin entered the offices of the British Admiralty.

"Ah, yes, Lady Jane," said the admiral, his face full of concern. "I am most honored by your visit. Do sit down."

"Thank you," said Jane. "I trust you know why I am here. Have you made plans yet for a rescue expedition to go after my husband?"

"Well, yes, that has been discussed," said the admiral.

"I pray you do more than discuss it," said Jane. "You know that the *Erebus* and *Terror* had a three-year supply of provisions. Those three years are now almost up. That means they could be stranded somewhere in that icy wasteland without food." She bit her lip, trying to keep away the haunting image of her husband frozen or starving on some desolate chunk of ice.

"I assure you, we shall do all we can," said the admiral. "Sir John has served his country well. I give you my personal guarantee that a rescue mission will be sent soon."

Soon wasn't good enough for Jane Franklin. She wanted to hear the word "now."

"I should like to go on the rescue expedition," she said.

The admiral coughed and spluttered in surprise. "My dear Lady Franklin! I admire your courage, but you know that is out of the question!"

"Why is that?" she demanded icily. "I have more at stake than any of you in finding these lost ships."

"But the hardships . . . ," started the admiral.

"I know all about the hardships," she said. "If my husband could be asked to bear them in the name of the crown, I would gladly do the same."

"I am sorry, Lady Franklin," replied the admiral. "But I cannot allow a woman on such a difficult expedition."

Franklin had known that. She resented the fact that she could never go on these voyages simply because of her sex.

Politely she thanked the admiral for his efforts. "Will you do me a favor, then?" she asked, pulling out a white envelope. Please have your rescue party deliver this letter to my husband."

The admiral's hand shook as he took the letter. He was almost certain they would have heard something from Sir John if he was still alive. This woman's fierce belief in her husband moved him almost to tears.

The British did send out an expedition that year, but it returned without finding a trace of John Franklin. The ships seemed to have vanished from the face of the earth.

"Send another expedition!" pleaded Jane Franklin. The British obliged her by sending a second expedition.

Beside herself with worry that the British were not handling the search well, Lady Jane sought other sources of help. She even wrote a letter to United States president, Franklin Pierce. The president wrote back promising his assistance.

Over the next several years, more expeditions were sent. Two ships sailed off. A land expedition trudged into the Arctic. Four more ships sailed. One of these ships was renamed Lady Franklin in honor of that woman's tireless efforts. But these expeditions, too, failed to find any trace of Sir John.

By this time, everyone had long given up hope that Sir John and his crew were still alive. Everyone, that is, but Lady Jane. She studied all his notes for clues as to where he might have gone. Thinking that Sir John might have made it nearly to the end of the Northwest Passage before running into trouble, she bought a ship and hired a crew to search from Russia, moving east.

One day, miraculously, her tremendous efforts appeared to pay off.

"Look at this newspaper story!" one of her friends cried, dashing in the door. Hands trembling, Lady Jane opened a newspaper and saw a headline in bold type telling of the discovery of the

Franklin expedition. Lady Jane cried for joy as she read the article about how the crew had been found alive, stranded deep in the Arctic regions.

But the report turned out to be a cruel hoax. No one had seen Franklin or his crew. After having her hopes raised so high, Lady Jane plunged into despair.

But, for the sake of her husband, she pulled herself back together. In 1856, she asked the British government for yet another expedition. The government put her off for nearly a year before Sir Charles Wood finally answered her.

"We have gone to great expense to discover the fate of your husband," said Wood. "We cannot justify spending more of the people's money on a search for those who are beyond saving."

"They are not beyond saving," Jane insisted. "Remember when John sailed on that expedition to Great Slave Lake? They were forced back by a blizzard. Indians raided all their supplies and they were starving. More than half the men died. But who made it home alive? John Franklin, that is who. Sir John is a survivor. As for the cost, I will pay for it myself. If I spend every penny I have, it will be well worth it."

"Look," said Wood, losing patience. "We do not see the wisdom in risking the lives of more men just to discover your husband's fate. Do you realize that several of our search ships got stuck in the ice and nearly had to be abandoned? We very easily could have lost more lives searching for people who are dead. The British government will send no more expeditions, and that is final."

"Then I will find him without your help," said Lady Jane.

Jane's efforts to organize another search expedition drew nothing but ridicule. The *London Times* described her latest search attempt as "preposterous." Even Jane's family turned against her. Fearing that she would waste all of her inheritance on this useless search for her husband, Jane's father cut her out of his will.

Jane lay in bed at night wondering if she really was as crazy as everyone made her out to be. Perhaps it all was just a waste of time. Surely, she had to admit, John could not have survived this long in the Arctic without someone finding a trace of him.

But she could not help herself. She loved her husband deeply and had promised before God to be faithful to him always. To her, that meant never giving up, even when things were hopeless. As long as there was the slightest sliver of hope that John needed her help, she would continue to look for him for the rest of her life.

Jane consoled herself by writing poems to her husband:

> *My Franklin dear, though long thou stay,*
> *Yet still my prayer shall be*
> *That Providence may choose a way*
> *To guide thee safe to me.*

In 1858, Jane spent thousands of pounds to organize yet another search party. For this voyage, she chose Captain Leopold McClintock as the leader. McClintock sailed well up into the northernmost islands of the Canadian territories and then dropped south.

At a large island called King William Island, McClintock found a mound of rocks that contained a metal cylinder. On the cylinder was a request, written in six languages, asking that the contents be sent to the British Admiralty.

The cylinder, which had been left by Sir John Franklin's crew, solved the mysterious disappearance of the Franklin expedition. Papers contained inside described how the *Erebus* and *Terror* had become stuck fast in the ice in early 1848. Despite exhausting efforts, the crew could not get their ships out. Weakened by hunger and scurvy, the crew gradually died out. Sir John Franklin survived until June 11, 1849, well after the first expedition had been sent to search for them.

Lady Jane thanked McClintock's crew by presenting each of them with a silver watch. After many years of anxiety-ridden days and nights, she could rest easy again. She had done her duty to her husband. Although she had failed to save him, she could rest in the peace of knowing what had happened to him.

To the end of her days, she cherished a letter found in the cylinder on King William Island—a letter that made all her efforts worthwhile.

"To the Almighty's care I commit you and dear Eleanor. I trust he will shield you under his wings and grant you the continued aid of the Holy Spirit. Again, that God bless and support you both is and will be the constant prayer of your most affected husband."

Although he did not live to see the fruit of his work, John Franklin did accomplish his mission. He had found a way through the Arctic regions. By traveling due west from King William's Island, a ship can complete the Northwest Passage across the Americas. Jane's efforts made sure that Franklin got recognition for this achievement.

Talk about It

- Why do you think Lady Jane refused to give up the search, even after there was practically no chance that Sir John was still alive? Considering what did happen to Sir John, was Lady Jane's long and costly search worth the effort?

- Why was Sir John's letter to Jane such a comfort to her?

Prayer

As a family, sing or say together the first verse of the hymn "What a Friend We Have in Jesus" to remind you of God's faithfulness to us.

Blank Spot
on the Map

ALEXINE TINNE
1835–1869

y the 1860s, adventurers had explored most lands on earth. Yet there remained a few blank spots on the maps of the world, areas where no foreigners had set foot. One of these was in Central Africa, where streams trickle out of a large swamp on their way to join the mighty Nile River.

Even the most daring explorers passed up the challenge of exploring this region along the River of Gazelles. All except one of the least likely explorers of all: Alexandrine Petronella Francina Tinne (tih-NAY). Before Tinne arrived in Africa, no one had ever heard of a woman leading an exploration. Women were rarely allowed to travel. When they did, it was under the protection of their husbands, fathers, or other male relatives.

Tinne, however, loved adventure. She was the daughter of a wealthy Dutch merchant who died when she was nine. Her father left his great fortune to her. Tinne started traveling as a way to get over her breakup with the man she had intended to marry. Spending the fortune left by her father, she organized trips to more and more remote parts of the upper Nile River. Eventually, she set her sights on the blank spot on the map.

PASHA STARED, BUG-EYED. Only politeness kept the official from the city of Khartoum from laughing out loud at what he had just heard. "You mean to take a trip up the River of Gazelles?" he asked. He knew Alexine Tinne better than to add what he was thinking: "You, a woman?"

Tinne smiled at his efforts to hide his amusement. She could hardly contain her excitement. "Of course we're going! We'll have a wonderful time. I can hardly wait."

"Did you say 'we'? Surely you don't mean to take your mother with you!"

Tinne said nothing.

"You have no idea what you are getting into," said Pasha, sweat starting to bead on his forehead. "The river is treacherous. The heat is unbearable. Many die of fevers and sickness—not to mention the wild animals and fierce tribes! Why, there are no maps of the area. You could easily get lost and starve to death!"

"Please, don't be such a worrier," Tinne said, patting his hand. "I'm going. And, of course, Mother is coming, too. How could I say no to her? Oh, I know there are risks. There always are on an adventure. But imagine walking on ground that no white person has ever seen!"

Pasha shook his head in dismay. He knew there was no talking Tinne and her mother out of anything.

Tinne loved to travel in style and comfort. She rented six boats for the first part of the journey. These she filled with food and supplies, plus hundreds of servants. The servants would carry all the supplies once the group left the river. In addition, a couple of German scientists eagerly joined the traveling party.

The ships had barely set sail when Tinne's servant, Anna, came running to her. "There's a leak! I saw it when I was down in the cargo hold!"

Tinne shrugged. "Not the best beginning to a trip," she said. The crew quickly made for shore. As they set about repairing the leak, one of the sailors called her over. "Look at the size of that hole!" he said, pointing to a gash in the wood. "If your maid hadn't discovered it, we'd be sitting at the bottom of the river."

Tinne angrily sent for the captain. "What is going on?" she asked. "I paid good money for this boat. The least I expect is a boat that floats."

The captain licked his lips nervously. "I am very sorry. I did not notice the leak."

"How could you not notice a hole as large as a bucket?" Tinne demanded. The captain's eyes darted around, but he made no answer.

Tinne sighed. "You are holding something back. Tell me what you know about this hole. The truth this time!"

The captain looked at her in fear. "Please forgive me. I made the hole. I do not want to go up the River of Gazelles."

"What are you afraid of?" asked Tinne.

"The people who live there are cannibals," wailed the captain. "They are devils with tails and they have eyes growing out of their armholes."

"Oh, I don't believe that for a moment," said Tinne. "Fine! If you do not wish to come with us, then go home. I shall find another captain."

Finding a captain who would sail up the River of Gazelles was not easy. By the time they finally left Khartoum, they were behind schedule.

The river was beautiful but frustrating. At one point, the water was a thick stew of floating plants that clogged the paddles of their boat. Once they found a wall of grass and sod a hundred feet wide standing in the way. The group spent several days cutting and digging through the mass so they could get their boats through.

By the time the group reached a lonely outpost called Mashra, they were very low on food. Tinne and her mother waited there while boats went back to Khartoum for more supplies. This delay would put them two months behind schedule. Tinne grew concerned. They would have to hurry to beat the rainy season. No one could travel in the swamps around the River of Gazelles once the summer rains began.

At last, the explorers left Mashra and headed into uncharted country. As Tinne had expected, the reports of fierce, demonish tribes had been false. They passed through many villages but found only peaceful people living in neat straw houses. Often, the villagers let Tinne and her mother sleep in their houses.

The servants, however, remained fearful. The tension of wandering in a strange land made them irritable. One night, a brutal storm struck. The winds blew so hard that Tinne's tent fell over. Blasted by wind and rain, she finally managed to get the tent back up and then collapsed into her bed.

The next morning, she crawled out of the tent to find a row of muskets aimed at her head. The servants holding those muskets said they had had enough of this miserable wilderness. They were going home.

Tinne ignored the muskets. "You all agreed to this journey," she reminded them. "I spent a fortune equipping us. How dare you back out! Put down those guns this instant!"

Impressed with her courage, the servants threw down their guns. One by one, they apologized to Tinne for their threats.

For weeks, Tinne and her mother enjoyed their travels through lush green lands. They marveled at the herds of elephants and buffalo that gathered by the water's edge. Tinne took notes and sketched trees covered with bright flowers and birds.

All went well until they came to the outpost of a slave trader named Buselli. Tinne hated slave traders and did not trust Buselli at all. Unfortunately, she needed to hire more porters to carry their goods across the soggy land to drier hills. Buselli was the only one who could arrange this.

Tinne made deals with the slave trader only to have Buselli break his promises. The porters failed to show up. Buselli raised his prices to ridiculous levels. By the time Tinne finally got free of the slave trader, rains had flooded the land. There was no hope of reaching the highlands until the rainy season ended.

As Tinne searched for a suitable shelter where the expedition could spend the next few months, disaster struck. Harriet Tinne, Alexine's mother, fell ill with a fever. Days later she was dead. All of Alexine's dreams of adventure and exploration were shattered. She hardly cared if she lived or died now. Numb with grief, she set out to carry her mother back to her homeland.

But travel through the rain-soaked land was nearly impossible. Tinne realized that they would run out of food long before they made it back to Khartoum. Her grand adventure seemed certain to end in death for all of them.

"Oh, Mother, I wish you were here!" she sobbed. "I don't know what to do! I just want to give up. I don't care anymore!"

But through her tears, she realized that the remaining members of the expedition counted on her for leadership. Hopeless as matters seemed, the group had no chance without someone to hold it together.

"God, please help me," she asked silently. "Help me to do the best I can for these people. Help me not to lose hope."

Day after day, the weary party struggled again to find the River of Gazelles. The heat, mosquitoes, hunger, and terrifying fever sapped their strength. But Tinne kept them going. "Soon we shall reach the village of Wau," she told them.

But she saw doubt in their eyes. So what if they reached Wau? It was nothing but a tiny village. They would not find enough food there to last them until they reached Khartoum. Tinne refused to think of what she would do then.

Shortly after they reached the straw huts of Wau, Alexine spotted a troupe of soldiers. These were not soldiers of local tribes; they appeared to be from far away. One of them approached her. "You must be Mademoiselle Tinne. Your Aunt Addy in Khartoum was worried about you. She hired us to come to your aid."

Tinne sank to her knees. "Oh, thank God!" she gasped. She was still too crushed by the death of her mother to feel joy, but she felt an enormous sense of relief. When things had looked bleakest, she had clung to hope. That had been enough to see them through. They were going to make it home.

On March 29, 1864, fourteen months after the start of their journey, Alexine Tinne arrived back in Khartoum.

She never returned to the Netherlands but continued to explore lands where few Europeans, and certainly no European women, had ever set foot. The hazards finally caught up to her. Alexine was killed by bandits in 1869 at the age of thirty-three while attempting to cross the Sahara Desert.

Throughout her travels, she displayed not only courage, but such cheerfulness and kindness that she was known among the peoples of the upper Nile as "The Queen of the Equator."

Talk about It

- Tinne's expedition suffered through one disaster after another. How successful was her exploration of the River of Gazelles? How would you describe Alexine Tinne: brave? foolhardy? stubborn? persistent? Is she a person you admire?

- Tinne was so crushed by her mother's death that, for a time, she didn't care what happened to her. What made her snap out of her depression? Did Tinne believe she was going to make it back to Khartoum, or did she only hope to make it to Khartoum? What is the difference between faith and hope? Why is it so important never to give up hope, even when things seem hopeless?

Prayer

Spend time individually and as a family talking to God about your hopes and dreams for the future. Ask God to be near you, to comfort and strengthen you in times of sorrow and disappointment. Finish by saying how much you look forward to being with God both in this world and throughout eternal life.